'An accessible and thought-pr(
and complex subject. This h
explore Scripture, search your
with the world around you.'
Helen Thorne, Director of Training and Mentoring, London City
Mission

'Andy Hartropp is well placed to write on economic justice with
doctorates in both economics and theology. He does so with care,
attention and insight. Andy is particularly strong in setting out a
biblical framework of justice rooted in God's character, built into
his created order and expounded for us in his written word. Much
of the ethical and other dilemmas in business derive from the inter-
action of these ideas. Andy is balanced, avoids the boxing of biblical
perspectives into the inadequate categories of 'left' and 'right' and
brings some welcome corrective to some of the overemphasis in
evangelical thought on the matters of jubilee. He relates this to the
world in which we live, the challenge of consumerism, high-interest
lending, the workplace and the role of the company. Economic
justice is a complex topic which Andy treats well and makes
accessible.'
Richard Turnbull, Director, Centre for Enterprise, Markets and
Ethics, Oxford

Andrew Hartropp is an economist, theologian and Anglican church minister. He has PhDs in economics (University of Southampton) and Christian ethics (Kings College London). His publications include *What Is Economic Justice?* (Paternoster). He is Associate Fellow of the Centre for Enterprise, Markets and Ethics.

GOD'S
GOOD
ECONOMY

To: Craig and Csillag

Happy reading
and learning!

Andy

ANDREW
HARTROPP

GOD'S
GOOD
ECONOMY

DOING ECONOMIC JUSTICE
IN TODAY'S WORLD

INTER-VARSITY PRESS
36 Causton Street, London SW1P 4ST, England
Email: ivp@ivpbooks.com
Website: www.ivpbooks.com

First published 2019

British Library Cataloguing-in-Publication Data
A catalogue record for this book is available from the British Library.

ISBN: 978-1-78359-764-2
eBook ISBN: 978-1-78359-765-9

Set in Minion 11/14pt

Typeset in Great Britain by CRB Associates, Potterhanworth, Lincolnshire
Printed and bound in Great Britain by Ashford Colour Press Ltd,
Gosport, Hampshire

Inter-Varsity Press publishes Christian books that are true to the Bible and that
communicate the gospel, develop discipleship and strengthen the church for
its mission in the world.

IVP originated within the Inter-Varsity Fellowship, now the Universities and
Colleges Christian Fellowship, a student movement connecting Christian Unions
in universities and colleges throughout Great Britain, and a member movement
of the International Fellowship of Evangelical Students. Website: www.uccf.org.uk.
That historic association is maintained, and all senior IVP staff and committee
members subscribe to the UCCF Basis of Faith.

Contents

Preface

This book is for anyone who is interested in having a *good* economy. When I say 'good', I mean something more than 'efficient' or 'growing'. If you ask an economist, 'Is the economy doing *well*?', you might expect an answer along the lines of 'Yes, national output is likely to grow by 2% or more this year.' But this book is about *moral* goodness in the economy.

I want to persuade you that *doing justice* is central to having a good economy. But I also want to show you that we need to rediscover what economic justice actually is. Lots of people like the *idea* of 'economic justice', but what if we are confused about what it means?

There may be a lot of surprises for you in this book. For example, the suggestion that 'economic justice' and 'God' have anything at all to do with each other may come as a surprise. But in that case, you should read on!

I am an economist, theologian and church minister. As a Christian, who has been thinking for more than twenty years about what economic justice is, I am convinced that God loves justice – including justice in economic life. So I also want to persuade you that the roots of economic justice are found in God and in his character. I want to share with you what I have been discovering about doing economic justice – on the basis of what God himself reveals to us in his written word (Scripture) and in the person of Jesus Christ.

Here is another thing that may surprise you: to *do* economic justice is – from my discovery – all about how we *relate* to one another in our economic dealings, such as buying, selling, working, producing and trading. So, doing economic justice involves all of us in our relationships. We cannot simply leave economic justice to the government.

There are also things in this book that may be *subversive*. For example, you may find that there are challenges to your own ideas of what a 'good economy' and 'economic justice' are all about. But I hope you will see that to be subversive is no bad thing if it leads us to a fuller grasp of what is good and true.

I would like to thank everyone who has helped me, in one way or another, in writing this book. I have interacted with lots of people over the past twenty years or more around the ideas of justice in economic life. Thank you to everyone who has challenged and encouraged me in those ways. Especially, I want to thank Michael Banner, Jonathan Chaplin and Donald Hay. I am very grateful to Philip Duce, my editor at Inter-Varsity Press, Eldo Barkhuizen, my copy editor, and to the people who have kindly commended this book – Helen Thorne, Richard Turnbull and Antony Billington. Thanks also to my father, Alan, and my children, Daniel, Rosanna, Bryony and Joseph, for all their promptings, proddings and encouragement down the years. Most of all, in human terms, I express my deep thanks to my lovely wife, Claire, my best friend, for all her wonderful support and prayers, and for being alongside me in all the ups and downs to do with this book, as well as in life generally.

Writing these words at Easter is a reminder that, in human space and time – as witnessed and written down – Jesus Christ lived, was publicly crucified and then rose from the dead. His resurrection tells us more clearly than anything else that every dimension of life really matters, including economic life. And so the good news that Christ came to bring is to impact upon every aspect of life, for both now and eternity.

Andrew Hartropp

Abbreviations

Introduction

What is this book about? A good way for me to explain is by telling you briefly about four convictions that underpin it: four key factors that have driven me to write this book.

Justice in economic life matters

Economic life – which includes buying and selling, employing and being employed – is not only about what is made, and how much is made: Gross Domestic Product (GDP) and all that. Having some economic prosperity is something to be very thankful for. But the *morality* of what happens in the economy is also very important. Is what is happening *good*? Is it *just*? I am convinced that justice in economic life matters.

Now there are questions about what 'economic justice' is. Chapter 1 looks at that in some detail. But economic justice is crucial. And, ultimately, the reason I am so persuaded of that is because of my second conviction.

God loves justice, and is just and righteous

I am a committed Christian. I believe and trust in one God, Father, Son and Holy Spirit. This God has revealed to us what he is like: we are not left to guess. God has given us his written word, the Bible (Scripture), which tells us that he loves justice. It also tells us that in his very being God is righteous, true and just. And the witness (testimony) the Bible gives us about God's *actions* confirms that he loves justice – and is also, wonderfully, gracious and merciful. But not only do we have the witness of what

Christians call the Old Testament part of the Bible; God has, even more wonderfully, revealed himself to human beings in personal, human terms – Jesus, the Word of God made flesh, come to this earth some 2,000 years ago as a human being. The New Testament is all about this Jesus and the good news (gospel) he announces. And the life, teaching, death and resurrection of Jesus reinforce in many ways that this God is just, merciful and gracious.

So I have a rock-solid basis for my conviction that economic justice matters. This is based not on my own (inevitably flimsy) reasoning, or on my own (inevitably fluctuating) emotions, but on the character of God himself. This is the just and righteous God who created and sustains our world and the universe. This world bears his stamp as its creator. That, ultimately, is why it makes sense to believe that economic justice matters.

The big picture of God's salvation plan: the kingdom of God

The Bible begins with the fact that God created the heavens and the earth (Gen. 1 – 2). Its final book, Revelation, looks ahead to when God will create a *new heaven and new earth*. This tells me that the material world matters to God. And, therefore, what happens in economic life matters to him.

Creation and new creation are like Act 1 and Act 4 in a play. What happens in Act 2 and Act 3? The Bible explains that human beings from very early on (Gen. 3) rebelled against God: they disobeyed his clear word and sinned. This rebellion is often termed the 'fall'. The fall, which is Act 2 in this real-life drama, and its bad consequences have permeated every dimension of life, including economic life.

But God did not leave humankind to rot. Instead, he acted to *redeem*. This is what 'salvation' is all about. God chose to call a people for himself: he redeemed (rescued) these people out of slavery in Egypt. And, ultimately, God came to this earth, as I have already mentioned, in the person of Jesus Christ, the Son of

God – in order to bring to fulfilment God's saving work. This is Act 3 of the real-life drama.

So the big picture of the Bible is a real-life drama in four acts:

Creation ⟶ Fall ⟶ Redemption ⟶ New Creation

I rejoice that God is the God of salvation. I am convinced his salvation plan is true and that he is working out this wonderful plan. I am convinced also that God will bring it to completion in the new creation. And I am glad that this work of redemption and salvation includes the material, physical and economic dimensions of life. Salvation is not confined to some 'spiritual' realm distinct from the created order: instead, salvation is taking place, and will come to fulfilment, *within* the context (framework) of creation and new creation.

When the Bible talks about *the kingdom of God*, this is another way of referring to this same marvellous salvation plan. God is sovereign over the whole universe. Since the fall, human beings have been disobeying God, rejecting his rule. But he has not left the situation like that. Instead, as I have already said, he has acted, and is acting, to bring redemption. The kingdom of God is God's *saving rule*, with Jesus Christ as God's anointed king. The kingdom of God is therefore *good news* (Matt. 4:23; Mark 1:14–15); and this good news (gospel) includes the fact that the God who loves justice will bring perfect justice to *economic* life.

Secularization is dominant in the Western world – not least in economic life

'One of the major reasons why people reject the Gospel today is not because they perceive it to be false but because they perceive it to be trivial.'[1] These words from John Stott sum up the massive difficulty presented for Christians by *secularization*. By 'secularization' I mean the process of separating religious ideas and institutions from the public sphere. To put it more bluntly, God has been pushed right to the edge of the table. Just watch or read the latest news: is there *any* sense that God is in *any* way part of it? God and Christianity seem trivial and irrelevant.

So people live their day-to-day lives and never seem to come across God. This is the secularized world of the West.

And in the *economic* aspects of life, secularization is if anything even more dominant. How many people in Britain, or the West as a whole, would think that *God* has anything to say about GDP and economic growth, or about *economic justice*?

But God is still God! He is still working out his salvation plan! We must not, then, be defeatist. And we must certainly not simply put up, passively, with his having been pushed to the edge of the table. Quite the opposite! Jesus Christ wants his followers to be *in* the world – yet not moulded by it. He prayed for this (John 17:15–19). And the way to respond to secularization is *to push back.* Being *in* the world means *engaging* with what is happening, including in public, economic and business life. It means being part of all this: getting stuck in. It means *doing good* in all the rough and tumble of life, from Monday through to Sunday. And part of this doing good is, I am convinced, *doing justice in economic life.*

Os Guinness, a key Christian thinker, has written marvellously and passionately about responding to secularization by *engaging,* for the sake of the gospel. In his book *Renaissance* he says:

> We . . . face a common challenge as followers of Jesus in the advanced modern world. *It is, I believe, that we trust in God and his gospel and move out confidently into the world, living and working for a new Christian renaissance, and thus challenge the darkness with the hope of Christian faith, believing in an outcome that lies beyond the horizon of all that we can see and accomplish today.*[2]

I am convinced that to do justice in the economic sphere of life is a vital part of this confident engagement.

And it is by living and working in the world – including in the economic dimension – that we will have greater opportunity to testify to people about the good news of Jesus Christ. Life and witness belong together.

But to live and work in the world require that we try to *understand* what is happening today. That is partly why I have written this book. Many people do want a greater measure of something called 'justice': but they really have very little idea of what this justice is, or where to find it, or how to achieve it! As followers of Christ we need to understand that; and we need to understand what God tells us in the Bible about economic justice. Hear Os Guinness again: 'one positive reason to understand the world is our desire to love the world too and to witness to the world, for the world is the social setting within which people hear what we have to say'.[3]

So, with my training in economics, theology and Christian ethics I have written this book in order to help equip you for this great task – of living and speaking for Jesus Christ in today's world. Doing economic justice is part of what God calls us to do, as part of living and speaking for Christ.

Structure of the book

In chapter 1 I look at a crucial question: *What is economic justice?* There is much confusion and disagreement here. But, as I will try to show, the Bible gives us a coherent and powerful understanding of what economic justice is – all rooted in the very character of God himself.

The rest of the book is divided into two parts. In part 1 I look at doing economic justice *in our relationships*: starting with us as consumers, and then moving out wider – in concentric circles, if you like – to the workplace, and to church communities.

In part 2 we will consider how we can do economic justice *in our wider society* – continuing to move out in a series of concentric circles. The emphasis in the second part will be on the role that followers of Christ can have *in and through* the organizations and structures of which they are part.

1

What *is* economic justice?

If you ask people, 'Are you in favour of justice?', most if not all will reply, 'Yes.' It would be unusual to find someone who says he or she supports *in*justice. But if you ask people, 'What do you *mean* by "justice"?', then you are more likely to get a wide range of responses. Is 'justice' about fairness? Or is it to do with just performance of one's moral obligations? Or is it about due reward and/or punishment? Or is 'justice' more to do with equity and perhaps equality?

There are dictionary definitions of 'justice' – although these are often quite lengthy. For example, the Webster online dictionary distinguishes four different aspects of justice.[1] And this complexity serves to support my suggestion that there is a wide range of views about what 'justice' is.

When we focus more specifically on 'social justice' and 'economic justice', then the diversity of opinions becomes stronger. Some people believe that justice in society must be based on *rights* – and often on *human rights*. Many of us probably have at least some sympathy with that idea. The United Nations 'Declaration of Human Rights' is a powerful statement along these lines. These rights are believed by many people to be in some way innate to one's very existence as a human being – irrespective of, say, ethnicity or place of birth or gender. We could speak, then, about the 'right to education', or the 'right to shelter', or to food and water. Social justice would, on this approach, have something to do with ensuring that these rights are fulfilled in reality.

Some other people, however, believe that justice is based on *needs* – which is not really the same basis as rights. Needs are often quite personal, quite individual – specific to someone's circumstances.

(Rights, by contrast, are defined – as noted in the previous paragraph – as being innate to one's existence as a human being and are *not* specific to one's circumstances.) People trapped in slavery are in desperate need and may well cry out for justice. A whole community is close to death because of a famine: they need food, and we might say that it is a matter of justice that their needs are met.

Confusingly, there is yet a third possible basis for 'justice': and this is *merit* or *desert* – what is merited or deserved. It is sometimes said, 'A fair day's pay for a fair day's work': this understands fairness or justice to be a matter of reward, merit, desert. There is also a (negative) flipside of this: justice as punishment. If, say, an employee or manager commits a crime – for example a financial misdemeanour – then we can speak of a just punishment: such as losing a job, or even being imprisoned. Someone receives his or her 'just deserts', as we might say.

So we have *rights*, *needs* and *merits*: three alternative foundations for justice. The problem is that these three are typically in conflict with one another. For example, consider any situation where there is some limit on available resources: should these resources be allocated to people on the basis of rights, needs or merits? That rights, needs and merits are *mutually incompatible* foundations for justice is clear when we take into account differences across the globe in relation to culture, climate, age and the stage of economic development.

All this presents us with a huge difficulty: if there is no agreement on what 'social justice' or 'economic justice' is, how can we agree with each other on how to move towards greater justice?

The intensity of this problem can be seen more plainly when we consider the political left–right spectrum. Political ideas and thinking on the left tend to pay particular attention to *rights*: so, for example, people on the left tend to regard large differences in income and wealth within a society as in some sense unjust. This is often because it is a rights-based understanding of justice that holds sway on the left. For example, if everyone has the right to the same share of national income, then it would follow that large inequalities in income are unjust.

By contrast, political ideas towards the right of the spectrum tend to pay more attention to *merit*; so it is thought that people who have a high income *deserve* that high income – the efforts of the higher-earning people *merit* the outcome: 'They have worked hard for their fortune, fair enough.' On this view, there is nothing unjust about large differences in income or wealth.

Can you see the problem? The two approaches are deploying entirely different, and mutually incompatible, ideas of what justice is. Who is to say which is better or more valid? How could anyone judge (so to speak) between them?

There is another way of seeing this problem. Over many centuries, when philosophers and others have thought deeply about justice – especially in economic life – they have often distinguished between, on the one hand, *justice in production or exchange* and, on the other hand, *justice in distribution*.[2] The problem – as I will explain shortly – is that when people think about 'economic justice', they often choose *one or the other*. So there is again no agreement on what justice is.

The first of these two categories, *justice in production or exchange*, focuses on whether there is any *exploitation* between producers and suppliers, or between retailers and consumers, or between firms and employees. By *exploitation* I mean something that is the opposite of justice. For example, suppose that in country X there is only one supermarket chain, call it 'Cheapsell' – there are no, or hardly any, competitors to Cheapsell. In this situation Cheapsell has such power in the marketplace that it is potentially able to exploit the suppliers of, say, food produce. It is in a position where it can force down to an extremely low price the amount it pays to suppliers – far lower than would be the case if there were some degree of competition between rival supermarkets. If Cheapsell utilizes its power in such a way, then farmers may virtually be unable to survive on the meagre amounts of money they receive. So Cheapsell has the power to exploit its suppliers: to behave unjustly.

We can easily imagine a similar situation between firms and employees: a large and powerful firm in one sector of the economy may be able to drive down to an extremely low level the wages it pays to its employees. (Assume for the moment that there is no minimum-wage legislation in that country.) Or, in (say) the market for electricity, if there is only one provider of electricity, then that firm may potentially be in a position to drive *up* the price of electricity that households have to pay, to the point where we can say, 'That's not fair!'

All of these can be seen as examples of *exploitation*: one organization, or individual, acting unjustly towards other people in the context of production, employment, exchange or trade.

The second category for justice in economic life centres on *justice in distribution*. Instead of the focus being on justice in production and exchange, this second category considers how income and wealth are distributed across the population. That is, rather than looking at the processes involved in making a cake, one looks at how the cake is shared out. In particular, the question asked is, 'Is this distribution *just*?' Is it fair? In particular, people often want to examine whether the share going to the poor is getting larger or smaller, and whether the share enjoyed by the rich is getting larger or smaller.

This second category – justice in distribution – may also make use of the idea of justice based on *need*, or sometimes the concept of justice based on *rights*. People often ask whether income is distributed in such a way that the needs of the poorest are provided for. Those who favour justice based on rights often assess whether or not the distribution of income and wealth is becoming more *equal*.

One of the striking features of the literature and debates about economic justice is that for many people it seems we have to choose *one or the other* option. We can focus either on economic justice as being about what happens in production and exchange, or on justice in distribution. But very few people seem to be able to think of 'justice' as embracing both of these aspects.[3]

It seems, then, that confusion reigns when it comes to 'economic justice'. There are several competing sets of ideas here. But the central difficulty here is how we are to *choose* between these varying ideas of what justice is. Do we simply have to 'pick and choose' – in the same way that we have to choose which shampoo to use, or which destination to favour for our next holiday? Who is to say whether justice should focus on production and trade, or on distribution? If we have the three options of rights, need and merit – as the foundation for justice – which is *true* justice? Can anyone say?

A pluralistic world

We have seen that there is a confusing range of options when it comes to trying to say what justice *is*. This confusion is connected to the fact that as the twenty-first century is unfolding, many societies are becoming more *pluralistic*. Whereas in previous eras it was common for there to be a dominant viewpoint in a society (e.g. about moral values or cultural norms), the twenty-first century is witnessing a large increase in *diversity* of viewpoints. This is pluralism. And this context of pluralism relates to the confusing range of options about 'What is justice?' in two contrasting ways.

First, in a pluralistic context it is much easier and more likely for a range of viewpoints about *anything* to emerge; and this includes options regarding 'What is economic justice?' Pluralism is a cultural seedbed that encourages all manner of opinions to take root and flourish. The flipside of this is that, in such a context, for any *one* viewpoint about anything (including 'What is justice?') to become dominant is much *less* likely now than it was in, say, Britain in the 1950s.

The second connection is that, for some people at least, a pluralistic approach to 'justice' is to be welcomed. For these people, it is a happy matter of 'Let a thousand flowers bloom.' 'You have your moral values and I have mine.' So you can have your view about what justice is, and I can have mine; and that is fine. Now it can become a little feisty when conflicts about justice come to the fore: person A may take, say, a very strong egalitarian view of justice, and work hard in the political arena to bring about policies that are intended to achieve far greater equality – on the basis that 'I believe that's what justice is.' If person B, holding a rival view of justice, disagrees, and therefore wants very different policies, then he or she will have to battle it out.

Lurking beneath the surface here is a well-established paradox: people who accept 'moral *relativism*' often hold their viewpoint with what looks like an *absolute* conviction. This seems to me to be a fatal weakness for the 'moral relativism' school of thought. A mainstream Christian perspective on this down the centuries is that there *are* moral absolutes, which derive ultimately from God. Many of these are revealed to us in the Bible, and this perspective is far more robust, in my view, than moral relativism.

To have some understanding of this pluralistic cultural context is very important – especially for someone like me. Why is that? I am a committed Christian who is convinced that the Bible is God's word written, and is to be accepted as both reliable in all it teaches, and as the authority, under God, for our faith and behaviour. In other words, I believe that what the Bible says is *true* – absolute truth. But the prevailing culture today in many countries pours scorn on this. ('Who are you to adjudicate on these matters?' 'Why can't you simply accept that each of us has our own legitimate viewpoint?') This cultural setting makes it much more challenging to present the view that the Bible can give us a *definitive* answer to the question 'What is economic justice?' But it is much better to be aware of this challenge than to be blind to it.

A biblical understanding of 'economic justice'

We have seen that there is a wide and confusing range of options when it comes to trying to say what justice *is*. We have also noted the pluralistic cultural context of the twenty-first century, and the challenge this presents. It is in all of that context that I come now to the task of presenting a *biblical* understanding of what economic justice is.

A framework for understanding justice

A crucial first step is having a *framework* for a biblical understanding of economic justice. There are three main elements to this framework, each involving a major claim (proposition). To put it another way, I am going to make three big claims – claims that will seem outrageous to some people, in a context of pluralism:

1 Justice – including economic justice – is rooted in *who God is*: in his very character. God loves justice, and is just in all he does.
2 God has built justice into creation. The world that God has created and sustains is a world that includes a *just order*. This is so especially for all of the ways in which *human beings* live and share in God's world.
3 The Bible – God's word written – *discloses to us* what justice is, and that includes justice in economic life.

Those three are big claims. The first is about the foundation of justice. The second is about an order – or structure – of justice. The third is about revelation – disclosure – of justice. These three claims (or propositions) provide the framework for *economic* justice.

Before I go on to present a biblical understanding of economic justice, it is important to say a little more about each of those three claims and about this framework. They are of such great significance that it would be foolish to rush on too soon.

1 Justice is rooted in God's character

This bold claim is very different indeed from how most think about justice. If you ask people, 'What is justice based on?', they may come up with a number of answers. One is that justice is some kind of abstract principle – an abstract *moral* principle, perhaps. Some people say that 'justice' is something we can *reason* about: justice is, then, ultimately in our *minds*. By contrast, to claim that justice is founded in *God's character* is a radically different approach.

On what basis do I say that God loves justice and all he does is just? It is because he has revealed himself to be like this, by his words and actions. Back in the Old Testament Moses is one person who saw God's actions, heard his words and responded as follows:

> I will proclaim the name of the LORD.
>> Oh, praise the greatness of our God!
> He is the Rock, his works are perfect,
>> and all his ways are just.
> A faithful God who does no wrong,
>> upright and just is he.
> (Deut. 32:3–4)

Do you notice what is said here? Moses declares that God *is* just, and that all his ways are just (v. 4).

Also, God self-testifies to the truth that he *loves* justice. Consider these words spoken through the prophet Isaiah:

> For I, the LORD, love justice;
>> I hate robbery and wrongdoing.
> In my faithfulness I will reward my people
>> and make an everlasting covenant with them.
> (Isa. 61:8)

To use the language of love in relation to justice is clearly a very strong statement from God; we would be right to say, then, that God is *passionate* about justice. This is deep in his nature.

One more example, for now, comes from the Psalms:

> For the LORD is righteous,
>> he loves justice;
>> the upright will see his face.
> (Ps. 11:7)[4]

Here we see the Scripture saying two things in combination: God loves justice and he *is* righteous. (By 'righteous' the Bible typically means that people or things are *true* to what they are, or should be: they conform to a standard.) God is righteous and true, and he loves justice. This is his character; this is who God is; this is what he is like.

The God who is revealed as being just and loving justice is the same God who created and sustains this world and universe:

The earth is the LORD's, and everything in it.
(Ps. 24:1)

So it should make enormous sense for us – as creatures who inhabit this earth – to realize that justice itself is rooted in the nature of this God. Justice does not come out of thin air. Justice is not a concept that we human beings have created by ourselves. No: justice is rooted in who God is.

2 God has built justice into creation

Here is a second bold claim, and the second part of our framework for understanding biblical economic justice.

When a team of engineers design a product – say a car – they ensure that a number of key features are built into the car. These features are *structural* for the car: they are necessarily part of it. One such feature might be the relationship between different parts of the car: the way those aspects interrelate. Another might be some innovative feature; for example, to do with the fuel system. When that car is manufactured and in time comes to be driven and enjoyed, those built-in features are necessarily part of it. There is an *order* to the construction of the car. It is in that kind of sense that I say that God has *built* justice into creation, and especially into the ways in which human beings live and share in God's world. There is an underlying *just order* to God's world.

I do *not* mean that everything being done in this world perfectly reflects this just order – any more than, in the illustration of the car, a person driving that car necessarily drives it perfectly, or makes proper use of its design features. Things in this world are evidently not perfect. By the Bible's own testimony there is in the present age much *in*justice. But the very fact that we can speak about *in*justice depends on there being an underlying feature or order of *justice*. Unless there were those design features in the car, it would be meaningless to talk about a driver failing to use those features properly.

I suggest to you that it makes great sense, intuitively, to say that God has built justice into creation. Why is it that when we see or hear about certain behaviours or situations, we cry out 'That's so unfair!', or 'That's obviously unjust!'? If justice is built into creation, and if we as human beings are part of that created order with some God-given sense of justice, then of course we might notice when things are unjust.

And this applies very much to social and economic life.

3 The Bible – God's word written – discloses to us what justice is: and that includes justice in economic life

This is the third bold claim I am making here. The first (see above) is that justice is rooted in God's character: God always does justice. However, it is one thing to assert that justice is rooted in who God is; it is quite a different thing to claim that we as human beings can know what justice is. But that is what this third bold claim is about. The God who is just has not kept to himself the knowledge of what justice is. Instead, he has chosen to disclose this to human beings. And the way God has chosen to do this is, centrally, by his written word, Scripture.

Words mean a lot to human beings – whether written or spoken or silent or signed or audible. Words are central in how we communicate. And Scripture says many times that it is God's word to us.[5] What I am claiming here, then, is that among the many other things that the Bible (Scripture) reveals to us is what justice, including economic justice, is.

This is a bold claim. Earlier in this chapter I argued that in today's world there is a confusing array of views about economic justice. But the *truth* of what economic justice is has been disclosed to us in *one* set of writings, the Bible. Many people today will respond to this bold claim by saying that it is either ridiculous or arrogant or both. Such a response, especially in a pluralistic context, is only to be expected. But that response in itself does not disprove the claim. And quite often the truth surprises us! If you are willing at least to give this claim a hearing, then perhaps you will consider the rest of this chapter as I set out the key aspects of a biblical understanding of economic justice.

Four key aspects of a biblical understanding of economic justice[6]

1 Justice means treating people according to the norms given by God. This is the core idea of what justice is, biblically. In economic life this means treating people in line with God's values for how we are to live in the economic dimensions of life. God has given his norms and principles in order for us as human beings to flourish.

Building on this central idea and definition, there are three further aspects to a biblical understanding of justice in economic life.

2 Justice includes an emphasis on how the poor and needy within a community, or society, are treated. Biblically, economic justice is not *solely* about justice for the poor and needy, but it does involve this as a special emphasis.

3 Justice is concerned with the quality of relationships. As we will see shortly, the norms given by God in Scripture very often address relational contexts; for example, buyer–seller and lender–borrower. And these often involve reciprocal (two-way) responsibilities and obligations. So justice is relational.

4 Justice in the allocation of resources means that everyone participates in God's blessings, including material blessings. In other words, in a flourishing and just community all are to share in God's bountiful blessings.

Let me now explain each of these in more detail, giving a flavour at least of the biblical basis for what is being claimed here.

1 Justice means treating people according to the norms given by God

There are a number of crucial features in this core idea of what justice is. First, justice is about *treating people appropriately*: so justice is something that we should *do* in relation to other people. Many times in the Bible we read about *doing* justice. In this book I will give a lot of illustrations of this, but at this point I think that one example will suffice: Genesis 18:19, where God ('the LORD') refers to his choosing of Abraham:

> for I have chosen him, that he may charge his children and his household after him to keep the way of the LORD by doing righteousness and justice; so that the LORD may bring to Abraham what he has promised him.
> (RSV)

Note that justice and righteousness must be *done*.[7] This reinforces the point that justice is about how we treat one another.

A good example of this, in an economic context, is what the Old Testament says about *just* weights and measures – used in selling and buying. Consider these verses from Deuteronomy 25:13–15:

> You shall not have in your bag two kinds of weights, a large and a small. You shall not have in your house two kinds of measures, a large and a small. A full and just weight you shall have, a full and just measure you shall have; that your days may be prolonged in the land which the LORD your God gives you.
> (RSV)

Note the emphasis on a *just* weight and a *just* measure.[8] We can picture the scene at a street market: someone wants to buy, say, some carrots and potatoes. The seller has a method for weighing the produce. The message from the verses above is clear: do not cheat the buyer by having weights and measures that result in giving the buyer too few carrots. So justice in buying and selling includes *treating* the other person in the right way.

Now some people might respond by saying, 'Well, that's obvious!' Perhaps it is. But do you think of proper weights and measures as a matter of *justice*? That is the point here. Biblically, this is one example of God's norms for doing economic justice.

A second example of norms concerns payment to people for the work they do. There is a cluster of biblical references here we will consider together. In Deuteronomy 18 God (speaking through

Moses) teaches the people about material remuneration for the priests. Now you might think that this is a very long way from our twenty-first-century context, but the key thing here is to note the *principle* given in these verses.

In verses 1 and 2 it is stated that the Levitical priests are not to have any land (inheritance) of their own – the reason given (v. 2) is that 'the LORD is their inheritance'. How, then, are they to obtain food? Verse 3 proceeds to answer that question by stating that when other people bring a sacrifice – for example an ox or a sheep – then certain parts of that animal are for the priests to eat. The text says (v. 3 RSV), 'this shall be the priests' due from the people'. The word translated here as 'due' is the same word often translated as 'justice' (*mišpāṭ*). So for the priests to be remunerated for the work they do is a matter of *justice*.

A related verse – also part of God's message given through Moses for the Old Testament people of Israel – concerns prompt payment of wages. In Leviticus 19:13 we read the following: 'Do not defraud or rob your neighbour. Do not hold back the wages of a hired worker overnight.' The norm here for proper and prompt payment is clear; and the opposite would be a form of fraud, oppression and injustice.

Moving into the New Testament, there is some significant teaching about wages, which comes in the context of how people who work specifically in *proclaiming the gospel of Jesus Christ* are to be remunerated. This teaching adds to our cluster of biblical references regarding payment for work done. In Luke 10:5–7 we read some instructions given by the Lord Jesus to a number of his followers as he sent them out on a mission:

> When you enter a house, first say, 'Peace to this house.' If someone who promotes peace is there, your peace will rest on them; if not, it will return to you. Stay there, eating and drinking whatever they give you, for the worker deserves his wages. Do not move around from house to house.

Note the statement 'the worker deserves his wages'. Now you might think this is an obvious principle, so why bother drawing our attention to it? To which I would simply respond that this principle may well seem obvious to many of us, but it is still important to point it out. Much of what the Bible teaches about economic justice is common sense – but sometimes our 'common sense' deserts us! The principle that workers deserve their wages is highly significant.

In his first letter to Timothy the apostle Paul applies this same principle to the work of leaders in a local church:

> The elders who direct the affairs of the church well are worthy of double honour, especially those whose work is preaching and teaching. For Scripture says, 'Do not muzzle an ox while it is treading out the grain,' and 'The worker deserves his wages.'
> (1 Tim. 5:17–18)

Note that Paul bases his statement here on two separate scriptures: the first is from the Old Testament (Deut. 25:4), and the second, strikingly, is the teaching of the Lord Jesus that we have just been discussing – Paul views Jesus' words as part of Scripture.[9] It is interesting how Paul takes a verse about how an *ox* should be treated and applies it to human beings! Paul is comfortable in recognizing that God's written word is logical, and expresses the mind of God. So it is perfectly reasonable to ponder on teaching about the right treatment of animals, and to derive from this teaching a principle for how we as human beings should treat one another.

The principle is clear: church leaders, especially those whose work is teaching and preaching, should be properly remunerated for the work they do. This is part of doing justice, part of treating one another according to the norms that God has disclosed to us.

We are on safe ground, it seems to me, to take this same principle and apply it to *all* human endeavour for which material reward (remuneration) is appropriate. In other words, the principle that workers deserve their wages applies to all types of employment. This is part of doing justice, part of how we are to treat one another.

So we have seen a couple of examples of what biblical norms and principles for economic life look like. These help to flesh out the foundational aspect of a biblical understanding of economic justice: that *justice means treating people appropriately, according to the norms given by God*. In the last couple of pages I have been highlighting one key feature of this definition, namely the way in which biblical justice is about *how people are treated*. Justice is what we are to *do*, especially in how we treat other people. We have also been considering a second key feature, which is the emphasis on *norms and principles* given by God.

Let me also emphasize, briefly, a third key feature of this definition: the norms and principles are *given by God*, who is the creator and sustainer of all things. This feature connects with one of the bold claims made earlier in this chapter, namely that God has built justice into creation. There is *a just order* to God's creation. And God has provided his norms for economic justice in order that we as human beings may flourish. To do God's will is always, ultimately, for our good – as well as also being for his greater glory.

Therefore God's norms and principles for economic justice are not in any way arbitrary. Instead, they fit with the grain of the created order. Now we as human beings are *commanded* by God to *obey* his perfect will – which includes adhering to his norms and principles for economic justice. However, such obedience is never, in the Bible, presented as obedience merely for its own sake. Rather, in obeying the will and commands of our loving God and creator we express our love for him in response to the love that he has first poured out on us;[10] and we also learn more and more to discover in practice that God's will is for our good.[11]

Therefore when (for example) we use *just* weights and measures, and in other economic dealings treat one another justly, then we discover that economic justice is a route towards human flourishing.

Having looked in some detail at the foundational aspect of a biblical understanding of economic justice, it is now time to consider, in turn, the other three key aspects.

2 Justice includes an emphasis on how people who are poor and needy within a community, or society, are treated

Biblically, economic justice is not *solely* about justice for the poor and needy, but it does involve this as a special emphasis. This is plain in many places in the Old Testament. A powerful and personal example is that of Job. Job was in the midst of great suffering, but in Job 29:14–16 we read how, as he anguished, he looked back to earlier days in his life:[12]

> I put on righteousness as my clothing;
>> justice was my robe and my turban.
> I was eyes to the blind
>> and feet to the lame.
> I was a father to the needy;
>> I took up the case of the stranger.

It is clear that wearing the clothes of justice – in other words, *doing* justice – involves acting to support the needy. This is a central aspect of doing justice and righteousness.

And this is no mere human invention. Instead, the ultimate inspiration and model for doing justice for the poor and needy is God himself. This is shown many times in the Bible. An example is in the Psalms:

> The LORD works righteousness
>> and justice for all the oppressed.
> (Ps. 103:6)

And in another psalm we read, similarly:

> I know that the LORD secures justice for the poor
>> and upholds the cause of the needy.
> (Ps. 140:12)[13]

In Jeremiah 22:13–17 God's commitment to justice for the poor is linked very powerfully to *our* responsibility to do the same – if we

claim to *know* this God. Through the prophet Jeremiah the Lord
speaks about Jehoiakim, king of Judah (see v. 18), whose father
Josiah had also been king. It is a severe message for Jehoiakim, in
view of the injustice he practised, especially in his economic
dealings. I quote the whole passage, so that we see the full context.
The key verse is verse 16 (italicized):

> Woe to him who builds his palace by unrighteousness,
>   his upper rooms by injustice,
> making his own people work for nothing,
>   not paying them for their labour.
> He says, 'I will build myself a great palace
>   with spacious upper rooms.'
> So he makes large windows in it,
>   panels it with cedar
>   and decorates it in red.
>
> Does it make you a king
>   to have more and more cedar?
> Did not your father have food and drink?
>   He did what was right and just,
>   so all went well with him.
> *He defended the cause of the poor and needy,*
>   *and so all went well.*
> *Is that not what it means to know me?'*
>   *declares the* LORD.
> But your eyes and your heart
>   are set only on dishonest gain,
> on shedding innocent blood
>   and on oppression and extortion.[14]

King Josiah 'defended the cause of the poor and needy, and so all
went well', declares the LORD. And the LORD continues (v. 16), 'Is
that not what it means to know me?'

Do you see the force of this? To know this God – to be in relationship to him – *means* defending the cause of the poor and needy.

22

And this in turn was a central aspect of doing what is 'right and just' (v. 15).[15]

One final example comes from one of the Old Testament prophecies of the coming Messiah (Christ). This is in Isaiah 11, which prophesies the coming of a man from the roots of Jesse, on whom the Spirit of the LORD will rest (vv. 1–2). Of this person we read the following (vv. 3–5):

> and he will delight in the fear of the LORD.
>
> He will not judge by what he sees with his eyes,
>   or decide by what he hears with his ears;
> but with righteousness he will judge the needy,
>   with justice he will give decisions for the poor of the earth.
> He will strike the earth with the rod of his mouth;
>   with the breath of his lips he will slay the wicked.
> Righteousness will be his belt
>   and faithfulness the sash round his waist.[16]

Those who have chosen to follow the Lord Jesus, acknowledging him as the Christ, recognize that in his life and ministry when he lived on the earth he indeed fulfilled this prophecy and the terms of this prophecy: Jesus Christ preached the good news to the poor, he called his followers to support the poor and he railed against religious leaders who *neglected* justice, mercy and faithfulness (see e.g. Matt. 5:3; 11:5; 23:23; Luke 4:18; 6:20; 11:41).

This, then, is a second key aspect of biblical economic justice: it has an emphasis on treating justly those who are poor and needy within a community.

3 Justice is concerned with the quality of relationships

This is the third key element in a biblical understanding of economic justice. The principles given by God in Scripture very often address *relational* contexts, such as buyer–seller and lender–borrower, and these involve reciprocal responsibilities. So justice has to do with relationships.

This emphasis flows directly from the core definition – explained earlier in this chapter – of economic justice as *treating people appropriately*, according to the norms and principles given by God. How we treat one another occurs in the context of relationships, and the thrust of this third aspect of economic justice is that the norms given by God address these two-way obligations.

An example of this comes in Deuteronomy 24. In this book we read how God, having rescued his people (Israel) from slavery, instructs through Moses how they are to live when they are in their new Promised Land. In Deuteronomy 24:17–18 we have some teaching on how the people are to treat the 'foreigner', who has come to live in the land given to Israel, the fatherless and the widow:[17]

> Do not deprive the foreigner or the fatherless of justice, or take the cloak of the widow as a pledge. Remember that you were slaves in Egypt and the LORD your God redeemed you from there. That is why I command you to do this.

Note again that God has taken the lead here in demonstrating how to treat people – he rescued his people out of slavery. So the people are to remember his actions towards them as they consider how they should treat others. They must not deprive these needy people of justice. What did such 'justice' look like? The very next verses (19–22) give a clear sense of this. They set out the principle of *gleaning*:

> When you are harvesting in your field and you overlook a sheaf, do not go back to get it. Leave it for the foreigner, the fatherless and the widow, so that the LORD your God may bless you in all the work of your hands. When you beat the olives from your trees, do not go over the branches a second time. Leave what remains for the foreigner, the fatherless and the widow. When you harvest the grapes in your vineyard, do not go over the vines again. Leave what remains for the foreigner, the fatherless and the widow. Remember that you were slaves in Egypt. That is why I command you to do this.

Here, then, justice means a clear responsibility on those who already have sufficient resources to enable those who do *not* have sufficient to be able to eat and live.

But there is also, if we study these texts carefully, a reciprocal responsibility on the part of those who are in need: the foreigners, fatherless and widows. They have to play their part, assuming they are physically able to provide for their needs, to go out and glean – to collect produce, in the way shown in verses 20–21, would involve effort on their part. (People who are infirm or too old to engage in such activity are cared for by the family/community in other ways.) Also, they are evidently *not* at liberty to harvest whenever and wherever they wish; instead, they must act within the parameters given by God. (This gleaning principle is also set out in Lev. 19:9–10.)

And in all of this there is a clear concern for the quality of relationships between people. Those who already have sufficient resources are to remember how *they* were treated by God, who rescued them out of their desperate circumstances; and they are then to treat those in need with the same kind of mercy and faithfulness.[18] This is all part of doing justice.

An important example of mutual responsibilities comes in the context of borrowers and lenders. What kinds of norms and principles does the biblical teaching give us here?

There is a lot of material in the Bible about this topic – discussed in more detail in later chapters in this book when we focus upon the practical application of biblical justice in today's world. For now, however, let me simply and briefly give something of the flavour of the biblical norms and principles.[19]

The key point is that there are obligations on both sides, and it is crucial to see that these are balanced. Consider these obligations in turn.

Borrowers have a responsibility to repay. This is a matter of justice. Psalm 37:21 states:

The wicked borrow and do not repay,
  but the righteous give generously.

To repay is not optional; *not* to repay is a feature of how the *wicked* behave. Whatever the reason for incurring debts in the first place, the borrower has a responsibility to repay the loan. In the Old Testament laws given by God through Moses there is never a suggestion that borrowers can evade their due responsibility.

But lenders also have serious responsibilities. Under God's laws given to Old Testament Israel through Moses one important responsibility was in a case where someone made a loan to a fellow citizen, and it was what today we term a *secured* loan – with some item or other (such as a garment) handed over by the borrower to the lender as a *pledge* or *security* ('collateral'). In such cases, there were clear constraints on the lender that protected the dignity and well-being of the borrower; for example, the lender could not enter the borrower's house in order to collect the pledge (see Deut. 24:10–11); and if the lender took a neighbour's garment as a pledge, then the lender could not keep that garment overnight (Exod. 22:26–27). So lenders had to treat borrowers with respect: this is an essential principle in the context of the relationship between lender and borrower.

A second major obligation for lenders under the Old Testament law was that loans to fellow Israelites had to be cancelled in the seventh year. This is made plain in Deuteronomy 15:1–11.[20] Such loans would typically be made only to someone who was in great need (as vv. 7–8 explain). In that context the obligation on those who had more resources was also to be generous, even if that year-seven cancellation date was fast approaching:

> Be careful not to harbour this wicked thought: 'The seventh year, the year for cancelling debts, is near,' so that you do not show ill will towards the needy among your fellow Israelites and give them nothing. They may then appeal to the LORD against you, and you will be found guilty of sin. Give generously to them and do so without a grudging heart.
> (Deut. 15:9–10a)

Behind these teachings we can see clear norms and principles expressing the will of God for how lenders and borrowers are to behave towards one another. Borrowers have a responsibility to repay. Lenders have a responsibility to treat borrowers with mercy and dignity; and, instead of lifelong servitude due to debt there is a principle of release and hence of *hope*. These teachings help us to recognize that economic justice is concerned with the quality of relationships, and the norms and principles given by God show us how we today are to treat one another in different relational contexts.

4 Justice in the allocation of resources means that everyone participates in God's blessings, including material blessings

This is the fourth and final key element in a biblical understanding of economic justice. In a flourishing and just community all are to share in God's bountiful blessings.

Quite a lot of what I have been saying thus far in this chapter has focused on how we should behave towards one another. This includes a recognition that a biblical understanding of economic justice includes a deep concern for justice for the poor and needy within a community. Under this fourth heading, however, the focus is more upon the *allocation of resources*. In other words, we are looking at how the 'cake' is shared out. What does the biblical material say about this?

The key point I make here is based primarily on the Old Testament teaching addressed to the people of Israel as they were about to enter the land promised to them. It is very important to recognize the context here – and especially the theological context. God had redeemed the people of Israel from slavery in Egypt. What was the responsibility of the Israelites here? It is spelt out plainly in, for example, Deuteronomy 11. Under the covenant (binding agreement) God had made with them he pledged to bring them into the land of promise. Under this same covenant *their* responsibility was to obey all the laws he was giving them. If they so obeyed God, then his blessings, including material blessings ('a land flowing with milk and honey', v. 9), would continue.

Now, since God had saved the people in order that they should be a holy *nation* (Exod. 19:6), and since he was bringing them into the land of promise, it was to be expected that *all* the people would enjoy God's blessings. Or, to put it negatively, given the context of covenant promise and covenant obedience, it was *inconceivable* that any of the people should *not* participate in God's blessings.

We see this principle worked out a little later in the book of Deuteronomy. There were three potentially vulnerable groups of people within Israel: the resident foreigners (or 'sojourners'), the fatherless and the widows. At that time none of these would have had any land (property) of their own. For example, if a woman became widowed, then the land previously held in the name of her now-deceased husband would pass to someone else (see Num. 27:1–11).[21] Did that mean that these people were prevented from sharing in the material blessings promised by God? Certainly not! Deuteronomy 16:11, for example, gives very clear teaching about one of the great annual festivals involving special worship services and great rejoicing, and about how the foreigners, fatherless and widows are specifically to be included:

And rejoice before the LORD your God at the place he will choose as a dwelling for his Name – you, your sons and daughters, your male and female servants, the Levites in your towns, and the foreigners, the fatherless and the widows living among you.

Note the inclusion of those three vulnerable groups of people.
The same emphasis comes a few verses later:

Be joyful at your festival – you, your sons and daughters, your male and female servants, and the Levites, the foreigners, the fatherless and the widows who live in your towns. For seven days celebrate the festival to the LORD your God at the place the LORD will choose. For the LORD your God will bless you in all your harvest and in all the work of your hands, and your joy will be complete.
(vv. 14–15)

Everyone is to participate in God's blessings, including material blessings. And this participation is not for festival time only, but for the whole year. Among various provisions made in the Old Testament law for those who were poor and/or vulnerable there was a requirement that, for every piece of land, a 10% share (a 'tithe') would be put aside every third year for these vulnerable groups. It seems likely that the 'third year' was specific to a given field – that is, in any given calendar year at least some fields would be in their 'third year'. This in turn would mean that in *every* calendar year food was coming in for these (potentially) vulnerable groups.[22]

What kind of provision was this? Was the amount a tiny (minimal) provision, or rather more? Consider the teaching about this third-year tithe:

> At the end of every three years, bring all the tithes of that year's produce and store it in your towns, so that the Levites (who have no land allotted to them or any inheritance of their own) and the foreigners, the fatherless and the widows who live in your towns may come and eat and be satisfied, and so that the LORD your God may bless you in all the work of your hands.
> (Deut. 14:28–29)

A key phrase here is 'come and eat and be satisfied'. The word translated here as 'satisfied' means 'filled'. Most of us know what a 'full meal' means! This 'satisfaction' is for *everyone*. And the provision taught here – with a proper system of storage, so that the produce could be accessed throughout the year – ensured that everyone would be filled all year long.

Note also that the emphasis here is not on some kind of numerical 'equality' but on *everyone*. Everyone is to participate in God's blessings, including material blessings.

This same principle was reinforced, for Old Testament Israel, by a range of other provisions; for example, compassionate loans for the needy (as we saw in the previous section); provision of housing and work for people who fell on hard times (e.g. Lev. 25:39–43); the *gleaning* principle (e.g. Lev. 19:9–10); and the promise of a grand returning of land, every fifty years – in the year of Jubilee – to the family group to which it had originally been entrusted (Lev. 25).[23]

In all sorts of ways, then, the Old Testament material teaches that everyone was to enjoy God's blessings, including material blessings. And this emphasis forms a key part of the norms and principles given by God, to show what it means to do justice in economic life.

Conclusion

In this chapter I have looked at how the Bible answers the vital question 'What is economic justice?' We have seen that a biblical understanding of economic justice focuses on treating people according to the principles given by God – which are all provided for human flourishing. Doing justice in economic life involves having a special eye for those who are poor and needy. It involves the quality of relationships. And biblical economic justice means that everyone participates in God's blessings, including material blessings.

With this foundation in place, the rest of the book – split into two parts – will build on it by looking at how all this can and should be worked out in life. Part 1 focuses on doing economic justice *in our own relationships*: as consumers, in the workplace and in local church communities. In part 2 we will consider how we can do economic justice in our wider society. The emphasis there will be on the influence that followers of Christ can have *in and through* the organizations and structures of which they are part.

Part 1

DOING ECONOMIC JUSTICE IN OUR OWN RELATIONSHIPS

2
Doing justice as consumers

I have just been watching a short video about a pair of trainers (well, it's an American video, so the chap called them 'sneakers') – not something I have ever done before! The video asked this question: 'What's the human cost of what I buy?'[1] For example, what are the working conditions in the factory, located quite possibly somewhere in Asia, where a particular pair of trainers were made? You might buy some trainers for £30, but what about the people who did the manufacturing in the factory – what is the cost *to them*? What is it like for them to work for whichever company makes the trainers?

The video, 10 minutes long, included some important information; for example, lots of factories that make items such as trainers have terrible working conditions: many of them use *forced labour* – that is, modern slavery. The video made the point that we, as consumers, are *connected* to the people who make things we buy. We may not know their faces, or see them day to day. But we are connected: we buy what they make.

Biblical economic justice, as we saw in the previous chapter, means treating people rightly in all our economic relationships, according to the norms and principles given by God – and that applies to indirect relationships as well as face to face. So we cannot duck the question and the challenge 'What is the human cost of what I buy?' And this is certainly the case for followers of Jesus Christ, who are required to treat people rightly.

Consumers in a global economy

A key idea here is the 'supply chain'. Businesses and economists use this term to refer to all the links involved in making, providing and then selling goods and services. Supply chains have become much more complex since globalization took off in the 1980s. Globalization means, essentially, a high degree of interconnectedness, economically, across the world. And this makes it possible for firms who manufacture any item, from trainers to smartphones to aeroplanes, to keep seeking out the cheapest and most suitable suppliers for *all* of the different components of their products – from anywhere in the world.[2]

Even a product as simple as a light bulb now has a very complex journey along its supply chain before it makes its way into your home. The same is true for many products in the contemporary world. Take trainers again: a particular new pair, for example, hit the market back in November 2016; and for this product, apparently, each trainer is made up of no fewer than 106 pieces.[3] This gives enormous scope to the company that owns this brand: conceivably there might be significant cost reductions and other benefits if it were to allocate production of these 106 items across a wide range of suppliers. For example, some suppliers specialize in – and are best at – making insoles, while others make the heels, and so on.

It seems likely that complex global supply chains are here to stay.[4] As with many aspects of globalization, it can be argued that there are both significant advantages ('upsides') from this, and significant disadvantages ('downsides'). On the negative side, even a well-intentioned producer of, say, trainers will not find it easy to check that all the different suppliers along the chain are providing decent working conditions for their employees. So the scope for exploitation of workers at many points in the supply chain is huge; and therefore the producer – based, say, in the UK or USA – will have to invest considerable effort, time and energy in ensuring that workers across the globe are not exploited.[5] The tendency for human beings, since the fall, to exploit one another is a fact, but globalization offers new scope for this malign downside tendency to operate.

On the positive side, however, globalization offers many advantages. In the case of global supply chains there are at least two major, and interrelated, benefits. First, products can be made cheaper, and brought to the marketplace speedier, than previously – which can benefit both consumers and producers. Second, the growth of manufacturing across the globe brings a huge increase in employment, and hence the opportunity for many people, for example, in Asia and elsewhere in the 'Global South', to earn a higher income than before and therefore escape from poverty.

But where does that leave us as consumers? If we – not least those who are followers of Christ – are to examine the human cost of what we buy, *how* are we to do this? You may be wondering, 'Are you seriously asking me to research into the morality of the complex supply chain for every item I am thinking of purchasing – before I buy it?' Well, that is clearly impossible; and I am not suggesting anything like that. But at least we can give some attention to this issue. We are connected to the people who make things we buy. And so we should give at least some thought to trying to treat people rightly. In a moment I will make a couple of simple suggestions for how we can go about this.

But first we must be clear: there is plenty of evidence of injustice in supply chains across the world. But let us again take the case of textiles and clothing. In that short video I mentioned earlier we are informed that '71% of fashion companies indicate there is probably slavery in their supply chains'.[6] Yes, 71%! More than seven out of every ten. This is very disturbing, is it not? Data will vary over time, but that one statistic should give us cause for deep concern. And slavery is not the only form of oppression in business and economic terms: it is probably the worst form (in the contemporary world), but many other people suffer under appalling working conditions, very low pay, and in other ways. So we must accept that there are extremely serious injustices here. Many people are being treated wrongly. And yet *we* may well have a connection to them: perhaps we buy what they make.

What, then, can we do? Here is one simple suggestion. A *possible* clue that a product might have been made with oppressively low wages further down the supply chain is if its price is substantially lower than any roughly equivalent item available on the market. Consider this to be an amber warning signal. This would certainly be a clue in relation to clothing: in the clothing/garment industry there is now a high degree of competition across producers, many of whom – notably in the West – are now committed to *avoiding* oppressive treatment of employees down the supply chain. That means that any firm which *is* charging a substantially lower price than anyone else may well be able to do so *only* by substantial *underpayments* to staff somewhere along the supply chain.

This would be only a warning signal: it would not be proof of anything. But, given a warning signal of that kind, one could then do a quick piece of research; for example, is evidence available through Internet sources that this company is consistently failing in its moral responsibilities to avoid injustice? If, having done that research, you are unsure about the morality of buying garments from this company, then perhaps you should shop elsewhere.[7]

A second simple suggestion – again making use of the information now so widely available online – is to give a bit of time, at least now and again, to looking up any evidence for companies that are widely seen to be failing in their moral responsibility for just treatment of employees, and for monitoring their own supply chains in that regard. Again, a quick search on the Internet – for example, using the words 'supply chain injustice', as already mentioned in endnote 5 – will offer a wide range of information. We can then take that information into account in our spending as consumers.

One remarkable feature of the Internet is that because of the information available a spotlight can be shone on the behaviour of companies, and that gives the rest of us considerable power to bring about change for the better. This does not require boycotts: it turns out that, such is the scope of online information and the number of people accessing it, individuals can work together and bring about change across the world.

So we can each play a significant part in doing justice – and in rectifying injustice – through how we spend the money God has entrusted to us.

The prophet Isaiah says:

Is this the kind of fast I have chosen,
only a day for people to humble themselves?

Is it only for bowing one's head like a reed
    and for lying in sackcloth and ashes?
Is that what you call a fast,
    a day acceptable to the LORD?

Is not this the kind of fasting I have chosen:
to loose the chains of injustice
    and untie the cords of the yoke,
to set the oppressed free
    and break every yoke?
Is it not to share your food with the hungry
    and to provide the poor wanderer with shelter –
when you see the naked, to clothe them,
    and not to turn away from your own flesh and blood?
Then your light will break forth like the dawn,
    and your healing will quickly appear;
then your righteousness will go before you,
    and the glory of the LORD will be your rear guard.
(Isa. 58:5–8)

This message, given from God through Isaiah centuries before the coming of Christ, reveals to us the mind of God on these fundamental issues involving human beings and on what God is looking for from his people. God's will has not changed. So let us give some thought to the possible human cost of what we buy, and then take action. In so doing, we can help to loose the chains of injustice.

'Ethical shopping'?

At this point some readers may be wondering, 'Is this writer talking about "ethical shopping"?' I would like to answer, 'Yes,' but in fact my answer is 'No'! Let me explain. First, I have deliberately put the term 'ethical shopping' in quotation marks. It is because of how this term has recently come to be used, in Britain at least, that my answer to my imaginary questioners is 'No'. I certainly believe that ethical values should guide our behaviour as consumers – and that is why I would *like* to answer 'Yes.' But it is the way this term has come to be used that makes me uneasy.

Second, then, let me say something about the usage of the term 'ethical shopping' – and other similar terms such as 'ethical consumer'. If you conduct an online search for terms such as these, you are likely to come across the following two things: first, an emphasis on some kind of 'ethical ranking' or 'ethical scorecard' – based, for example, on information about the behaviour of the producer regarding the environment, animals and people; and political factors; and, second, a facility whereby individuals can tailor their own ethical scorecard of producers, according to *their own* 'ethical preferences'.[8]

Although there are some helpful aspects in all this, my core criticism of an 'ethical shopping' emphasis is that it *reduces* the word 'ethical' to an exercise in *measurement*. The idea that one can *measure* or *rank* ethical conduct is never found in the Bible. God undoubtedly has a standard by which he assesses our lives, but that standard is his perfect love! 'You shall love the Lord your God . . . and your neighbour as yourself' (Luke 10:27 RSV). And God does give us a rank: 'all have sinned and fall short of the glory of God' (Rom. 3:23 RSV). Our score is, 'You have fallen short.' But God never offers us a *measurable* score; and he never suggests that we should *rank one another*. Even more problematic is the idea that people can have *their own* 'ethical preferences'. This is moral relativism. The Bible, by contrast, tells us that only God sets the moral standard for us. These criticisms lie at the heart of my critique.

This critique applies to both of the features I identified above in 'ethical shopping'. In any attempt to *measure* behaviour, what people or companies do must be reduced in some way. If you like, it becomes a 'tick box' exercise: someone sends out forms, or carries out an assessment using categories, but these are human constructs. Inevitably, they oversimplify: they reduce the reality to something that can be measured. This links to the second feature: to the attempt to *compare* different organizations and companies. Ranking requires a common and measurable 'score'. But, as I noted in the previous paragraph, the Scriptures never suggest that we as human beings should compare other human beings according to our own measure of 'morality' or 'goodness'. And moral relativism – which underlies the idea of having one's own ethical preferences – is indefensible, according to the Scriptures.

All of this critique can be restated in a more positive vein: in the Scriptures we see, consistently, a clear emphasis on 'Do justice' and 'Cease your injustice.' (We have already seen a number of examples of this, both in the previous and the current chapter.) This seems a much more attractive vision than that of an 'ethical scorecard'. Further, the Bible never says, 'Do a little bit more justice'; instead, it gives us a clarion call to do what is just in God's sight.

So it seems to me that the 'ethical shopping' emphasis is deeply flawed. And that is why I am *not* using that language or that approach.

No doubt there are useful things we can learn, if we take a look at how the 'ethical scorecard' approach attempts to evaluate different companies. We may well glean some useful information from 'ethical shopping' websites about some corporations, which may suggest that we should avoid buying from certain companies. But the deep flaws in the overall 'ethical shopping' approach remain.

A bigger idea of doing justice

Despite my critique of 'ethical shopping', one of the merits of that approach is that it draws attention to the moral responsibilities of consumers, and suggests that these responsibilities are quite broad. This does fit, to some extent, with the emphasis given at the beginning of this chapter, namely that we as consumers are *connected* to the people who make things we buy. 'Ethical shopping' can help here. How? By focusing attention on whether or not producers and retailers ensure that people all the way down the supply chain are not exploited. And that is, as already argued in this chapter, a key aspect of doing economic justice. The weakness of 'ethical shopping', as I have been claiming, is the way that it reduces this to an exercise in measurement. Justice is much bigger than that! And to do justice as consumers is a weightier thing than can be captured by any exercise of 'ethical shopping'. So in this section of the chapter we are going to consider some other aspects of what it means to do justice as consumers.

Subverting the dominance of 'consumerism'

But the first task here is for us to ask some hard questions about what it means to be a 'consumer' – and to subvert or at least critique today's emphasis on 'consumerism'. Someone may ask, 'What has this to do with economic justice?' It is fundamental.

In Matthew 6 Jesus Christ presents us with a stark choice. In verse 24 he states (in the NIV 2011 translation), 'No one can serve two masters . . . You cannot serve both God and Money.' 'Money' in the NIV 2011 is given with an upper case 'M' because this captures the idea of an alternative god. (It translates the word 'Mammon' from the original.) We cannot serve *both* the one true God *and* this rival god, centred on money and material possessions. 'Consumerism' – which includes a deep preoccupation with acquiring consumer goods and services – is a rival god. We cannot serve both God and consumerism. It is one or the other.

In the following verses Jesus explains further this stark choice that we all face: *either* we focus our minds and hearts on our physical life, our material needs and clothing (and 'run after all these things', v. 32), in which case we will inevitably spend time *worrying* about all of this; *or* we 'seek first his kingdom and his righteousness' (v. 33). To seek God's righteousness includes seeking his justice. We face, then, a choice between, on the one hand, consumerism and a love of money, or, on the other hand, love for God and a seeking of his justice. That is why subverting consumerism is fundamental to doing economic justice.

Let me say a little more at this point about the way that seeking God's righteousness includes seeking his justice. In the Bible there is often a close connection between doing *righteousness* and doing *justice*. We saw a number of examples of this in chapter 1. In the Old Testament, righteousness and justice are so closely tied together that we can view them as *one* reality.[9] It is the same as when someone says, 'I love restaurants and eating out': 'restaurants' and 'eating out' are not two separate things! They belong together. The importance of the one idea is reinforced by the use of the two words, each bringing out a slightly different emphasis. So it is with righteousness and justice. *Righteousness* emphasizes the inner quality (character) of doing what is right, being in line with God's will; and *justice* emphasizes the action of doing what is just.

In the New Testament in the original Greek normally only one word is used for 'justice' or 'righteousness', but the meaning of this one word often includes both aspects of being in the right and doing what is just/right. In the English language it is quite easy for us to slide over from 'being righteous' to 'doing justice'. For example, in the apostle Paul's letters to the Romans and the Galatians he writes a lot about how God, amazingly, *justifies* (declares just/righteous) the ungodly; this is on the basis of what Christ did on the cross – taking on himself the just punishment we as sinners deserved – and of Christian believers having a *righteousness* that is by faith. But in the Greek there is – as I say – simply *one* word (or one set of related words), sometimes translated as 'righteous' or 'righteousness' and sometimes translated as 'just' or 'justified'.[10] So when we read that we are to seek first God's kingdom and his righteousness, we will do well to be aware that 'seeking his righteousness' very much includes seeking to do what God says is just.

Jesus Christ tells us, then, that we face a choice: either we love money and consumerism or we resolve to love God above all else – which will mean a commitment to seek first his kingdom and his justice (righteousness). This is why I am arguing that to subvert consumerism is fundamental to doing justice, including economic justice. Unless the rival god of consumerism is dethroned *and* replaced by a determined and passionate commitment to love God above all else, then to do economic justice with any sustained persistence is impossible. Our hearts will simply be in the wrong place.

Being 'consumers': rights and wrongs

Another crucial aspect of learning to do justice is to get our thinking straight about being 'consumers'. The Bible is clear that 'God . . .

richly provides us with everything for our enjoyment' (1 Tim. 6:17). This gives a positive approach to material goods, food, sport and everything else in this wonderful world that God has created. The problem with 'consumerism', as I have been arguing, is that it puts these things *in place of God*. So we must view consumerism very negatively. But how are we to hold together, at the same time, a *positive* outlook on material things and a *negative* attitude towards consumerism and 'the love of money'? The first step is to appreciate that we must hold together both the positive and the negative. We will then discover that there are rights and wrongs to weigh up every day. But to make these daily choices, as consumers, is essential if we are to do economic justice.

Economists often argue that the behaviour of people as consumers is highly influential on the way that an economy operates. (The positive outlook noted just now, given in biblical and Christian thinking, is, happily, compatible with this emphasis.) One way to understand this impact is by noting that 'demand and supply' are at the core of much economic analysis. (I now offer you a short piece of such analysis – please do not walk away at this point!) This emphasis on demand and supply is crucial both at the 'macro' level (e.g. in the behaviour of a national economy as a whole – macro-economics) and at the 'micro' level (as in the behaviour of one market or industry, such as the market for bread – microeconomics).

The choices that consumers make – what they buy and do not buy – help to determine the overall demand for any service or product (such as bread). This demand will depend on a wide range of factors, including the price of the product (e.g. bread). On the other side of the market we find those who supply goods and services; for example, farmers, manufacturers and retailers. Again the supply of any product or service is influenced by a wide range of factors, including the price.

In practice, demand, supply and price interact in various ways, whether simple or complex. The result is that, broadly speaking, demand and supply are kept in line with each other; and the outcome is that you and I are able to buy goods and services, and those who supply them are able to make a living. But consumers are in general in a powerful position in this whole process, according to mainstream economic analysis. For example, if consumers overall (in aggregate) spend less on a type of bread, then this fall in demand will typically lead both to a fall in sales of bread and a fall in the price of bread. (Markets for goods and services are constantly adapting in order to bring demand and supply closely in line with each other.) Consumers are in this way able to send 'signals' to suppliers.[11]

Is all this positive? The Bible teaches, as noted already, that God richly provides us with everything for our enjoyment. Given that perspective, it seems to me a good thing if we have an economic system in which individuals and households have the freedom to exert influence on producers through choices.

At the same time, however, an awareness of the power of 'consumerism' should alert us to the constant danger that our choices as consumers are in turn being influenced by a set of values that are far removed from the values of God's kingdom and his righteous justice. So we have to combine a positive perspective (on being consumers and on enjoyment of God's good gifts in creation) with a deeply negative (critical) attitude towards consumerism. To get our thinking straight about all of this is not easy: we must work hard at it.

How are we to do this, in practice? A vital thing here is to allow *God's values* to shape our thinking and emotions. This is where justice and righteousness can come in. If *these* values shape our thoughts and desires, then we will have a very different outlook on what to buy, compared to people whose desires are shaped by the power of consumerism. Let us think next, then, about some ways to do this.

Let justice influence what you buy

We have already seen that consumers can have a big impact on economic justice. So let us use that power for good! Followers of Jesus Christ are stewards of the money and other material resources that God has entrusted to us. As stewards and consumers we have

43

the potential to let justice influence what we buy; and in turn that can have an impact for good.

Part of being wise trustees is that we do not waste our money. So it is sensible to shop around, where possible. (Why pay more for something when you can pay less for the same item and same quality?) That is not a uniquely biblical insight, obviously: you do not have to be a Christian to be a money-saving adviser! But alongside that aspect of wise stewardship, we can also let justice influence what we buy. For example, we saw in the previous chapter that doing justice, biblically, includes doing justice for the poor and needy: a central aspect of justice. So we should look at how concern for the poor and needy can influence what we buy.

But how can we do this? I cannot possibly give a detailed guide here; however, we can all begin to use our imagination and explore some options. For example, many individuals and households do have some *discretion* in what money they have available for spending. What do I mean by that? I am referring to money that is available *after* paying for all the regular things; for example, mortgage/rent, food shopping, cleaning materials, gas/electricity, phone. It is sensible to apply normal money-saving criteria to all these regular items. And there may not be many obvious ways in which concern for the poor and needy can influence our spending on these items.[12] However, having paid for all these regular items, there may be some money left over, and this is where we may have scope for *discretion* and creativity. I realize that for *some* individuals and households money can be extremely tight, and therefore they have no discretionary money available. That presents a challenge for *other* households – to try to consider how to support and empower those who are needier. But plenty of individuals and households do have discretionary funds; and so let us think of creative ways of doing justice with these funds.

For example, during recent years in the UK and elsewhere a new type of business enterprise has developed: 'social enterprise'. A social enterprise can be defined as 'a company whose core mission is to benefit and improve society – be that via the community or environment. However, unlike a charity, it is still a business looking to run and grow independently and make a profit.'[13] Is it possible that some of the things you would like to buy are available from social enterprises? Are there some social enterprises whose approach to seeking to 'benefit and improve society' is an approach that you want to support? The only way to answer these and other relevant questions is to have your eyes open and do a bit of investigation!

There may, for example, be a Christian-run social enterprise that seeks to provide employment for people who have struggles of one kind or another – the poor and needy who have found it hard or impossible to gain employment elsewhere. Could you investigate some options?

This would be one way for justice to influence what we buy.

An attractive feature of social enterprises, by the way, is that their desire to make some profit is likely to help ensure that they are run efficiently. They will probably manage their resources well, and make a decent product at a competitive price. This means that if we buy from them, we are not having to subsidize inefficiency 'for a good cause'. Being in a marketplace provides a useful discipline.

Justice and our priorities as consumers

Once we start thinking along the lines of the last few paragraphs – allowing justice to influence how we use 'discretionary' money – it may be that God's righteousness and justice will begin to reshape our priorities as consumers. The more we give careful thought to doing justice as consumers, the more we will be enlightened about the ways in which the consumerist culture around us has been shaping our thinking and desires; and the more we will then be empowered to withstand the seductions of consumerism, and instead act on the basis of different priorities.

In writing this it is not my aim to tell readers exactly how much to spend, or precisely what to buy. Each of us is accountable to God for these things, and only to God. And this God has given, to all who follow Christ, wonderful gifts to help us in all this: the Bible, prayer, his indwelling Holy Spirit, and the mutual support and fellowship available as part of his church – the body of Christ. Do you ever pray about the money you spend? If not, then start this week!

A final thing to say, in relation to our priorities as consumers, is about *how much* we spend, save, lend and give away. (You might have noticed that I have not said anything about this until now.) As we allow God's righteousness and justice to affect our thinking and behaviour as consumers more and more, it may be that we will make some changes here also. Certainly, it is *not* a priority of consumerism to encourage us to look out for the poor and needy: far from it! Again, however, I have no desire to make recommendations. How much we spend, save, lend and give is up to each of us, before God.[14] That principle is made plain in the Scriptures, notably by the apostle Paul. As he wrote to the Christians in Corinth (2 Cor. 9:7), 'Each of you should give what you have decided in your heart to give, not reluctantly or under compulsion, for God loves a cheerful giver.'

How we as consumers treat people

Part of doing economic justice biblically is treating people appropriately *in our relationships*. We are to behave rightly towards others, according to the norms and principles given by God in his word. We saw this in the previous chapter. So let me ask you a question. When you go shopping, how do you view the people who serve you?

In a consumerist culture driven by 'me first' (or 'me and my family first'), it is all too easy for us – even as followers of Christ – to be influenced by that culture. It is the cultural air that we breathe much of the time. For a 'me first' shopper, it is not a problem at all to be rude to a customer-service assistant. Why is that? Because 'shopping is about me'; and so such a shopper is quite likely to view people who work in a shop merely as tools to 'my satisfaction'.

By contrast, to do economic justice, as consumers, involves treating rightly every person with whom we come into contact. This is a mindset that is totally opposed to that of the prevailing consumerist culture. So there is a full-on clash here.

Now plenty of people, not only Christians, as consumers and customers still seek to be polite. Increasingly, however, it seems that a 'me first' culture is taking over in both the retail and service sectors. For example, organizations now sense the need to display posters saying things along the lines of 'Abuse of staff will not be tolerated.' This was not the case, say, back in the 1980s in the UK.

It also seems more and more that to be courteous is an option, rather than an obligation: if customers are treated well, they may be polite in response; but plenty of customers think that they can be rude if they do not get their way.

It should not be like this, however, for followers of Jesus Christ. We have an obligation before the Lord to treat people with kindness and patience irrespective of how they treat us. In his first letter the apostle Peter, citing Psalm 34 from verse 10 onwards, puts it this way:

Do not repay evil with evil or insult with insult. On the contrary, repay evil with blessing, because to this you were called so that you may inherit a blessing. For,

Whoever would love life
    and see good days
must keep their tongue from evil
    and their lips from deceitful speech.
They must turn from evil and do good;
    they must seek peace and pursue it.
For the eyes of the Lord are on the righteous
    and his ears are attentive to their prayer,
but the face of the Lord is against those who do evil.
(1 Peter 3:9–12)

These verses tell us plainly what it means to be *righteous* (or *just*): we are to do good and seek peace with other people.

Now in my own experience there are times when, as a customer, I have to be – let me say – *assertive*. If we have a valid complaint, then it is proper for us to air that complaint and seek due resolution. The Scriptures give us plenty of examples of standing firm against people who would malign the people of God; for example, the apostle Paul in Acts 16:37. However, firmness is always to be accompanied by grace, a gentle spirit and a humble heart. All of this is part and parcel of treating other people according to the norms and principles given by God in his word, which gives us much teaching on how to treat other people rightly. I quoted above from one of Peter's letters, who in turn quoted from one of the psalms. There is much material, in both the Old and New Testaments, to help us know how to live in a way that pleases God. But we must devote ourselves to feeding on the word of God. Jesus shows us this plainly – for example, see Matthew 4:4. In order to resist the prevailing consumerist culture we must spend much time in learning the counterculture of living as God's people.

Conclusion

If we want to do economic justice – according to biblical teaching – then it will have a big impact on our behaviour as consumers. It will affect how we treat other people with whom we have a connection as consumers. This is part of what it means to be followers of Jesus Christ: people who are living by faith in him, and are learning to love God above all else; people who are seeking first the kingdom of God and his justice.

In the next chapter we will look at a second area where doing economic justice will have a major relational impact: our relationships in the workplace.

3

Doing justice in the workplace

What is your preferred management style? Most if not all of us will have an opinion about that – whether we are managers, or are managed, or both. An online search will reveal, not very surprisingly, a wide range of different styles of management. Some experts give a list of six main styles, ranging from, for example, 'directive' to 'visionary' and 'participative' ('democratic').[1] But how many of these include the requirement to *treat people fairly*?

What about your attitude to work? There is, if anything, even greater variety here. The British Social Attitudes Survey is conducted in the UK annually, surveying over 3,000 people. This survey has been asking people whether they agree or disagree with the statement 'A job is just a way of earning money.' In 2015 49% said that they *agreed* with that statement. And over time there has been a high degree of consistency about that: throughout the period 1993–2015, 45–49% of people surveyed said they agreed with that statement.[2]

What about you? Would you say that a job is only a way of earning money? Can it not be part of doing justice and righteousness?

In this chapter I will consider how we, as Christians, can do justice in the workplace. Having looked in the previous chapter at doing justice as consumers, we will now move to the next of our concentric circles: moving outwards from what we *spend* – as individuals and households – to our relationships and behaviour in the places where we work. A later chapter will look at the wider influence for economic justice that we can have *in and through* the companies and organizations for which we may work. But this chapter focuses on doing justice in our own behaviour and relationships in the workplace.

Biblical themes

First, let me give a brief recap on a biblical understanding of economic justice. 'Justice' means treating people appropriately, according to the norms given by God. This includes an emphasis on how people who are poor and needy within a community (or society) are treated. We have seen also that economic justice is concerned with the quality of relationships. And justice in the allocation of resources means that everyone participates in God's blessings, including material blessings. But how does all this play out in the world of work? That is the heart of this chapter.

A second biblical theme is the importance of work itself, in God's big picture. In the Bible 'work' means activity – especially, purposeful and productive activity. (Work may or may not be *paid*.) And for human beings to work is part of our calling as stewards (trustees) of God's created world (see e.g. Gen. 1:28; 2:15).[3]

Therefore, work – purposeful and productive activity as stewards of creation – has a central place in God's big picture. Redemption never means any kind of escape from God's created order: quite the opposite. Redemption means, among many other wonderful things, *restoration* of creation from the damage done because of humanity's fall (rebellion against God). This restorative work begins in the present age: and we look forward with joy to the fullness of the restoration in the new creation that God will bring at the end of this age – when Christ comes again as judge, and every tongue will confess that Jesus Christ is Lord, to the glory of God the Father (Phil. 2:11). In the meantime our work is one of the arenas in which Christian believers, being transformed by the Holy Spirit into the likeness of the Lord 'with ever-increasing glory' (2 Cor. 3:18), are to display and work out this transformation: 'whatever you do, do it all for the glory of God' (1 Cor. 10:31).

Stark contrasts with today's culture

Before we look further at the biblical teaching on doing justice in the workplace, it is important to pause in order to note the radical contrast between the biblical picture of work, as sketched above, and today's dominant mindset and culture regarding work. If we want to apply the Bible seriously in our lives, we must understand our context today.

As I reported earlier, almost half of the people in Britain (in surveys) agree with the statement 'A job is just a way of earning money.' Now obviously that still leaves just over half who *do not* agree with that statement. So I must not make incorrect generalizations. But that survey evidence seems to reflect a wider feature of today's culture – for many people, work is about meeting *my* needs, attaining *my* goals, fulfilling *my* career plan and earning money for *my* leisure time. This reflects, in turn, the 'me-first' self-centred approach that has come to dominate British and Western culture.

There is a stark contrast between how this culture views work and the biblical picture of work. Have you grasped how great this contrast is? Yet it is in this culture that we live. Either this culture will take us over, or we must resist its influence upon us.

Underlying this culture ('the way we do things around here') is a mindset, a way of thinking, that both assumes and endorses self-centred individualism. This mindset has come to dominate *academic* approaches to economics and economic life. The situation is expressed well in the following quotation from a recent book by American authors Michael Rhodes, Robby Holt and Brian Fikkert: 'In the West, our prevailing economic worldview sees people as self-interested individuals with limitless desires in a limited world, who seek to increase consumption and leisure by earning as much money as possible.'[4]

These authors point out that this cultural world view is under-pinned by academic thought. They invite readers to consider the following definition of the academic discipline of economics, taken from a popular introductory textbook: 'Economics is concerned with the efficient use or management of limited productive resources to achieve maximum satisfaction of human material wants.'[5]

Many other similar definitions of economics exist. The phrase that should concern us is the last one, 'to achieve maximum satisfaction of human material wants'. This is a very long way from the biblical vision of stewarding *God's* resources to *his* glory under the rule of Christ. It is fine, as the above statement says, to seek efficient management, and resources are indeed limited, but the goal – maximum satisfaction of human material wants – is utterly wrong and foolish, according to the Scriptures. Consider, for example, the parable taught by Jesus Christ concerning 'the rich fool' (Luke 12:13–21), where the ground of a certain rich man produced a good crop. Having run out of room to store it all, the man said:

> I will tear down my barns and build bigger ones, and there I will store my surplus grain. And I'll say to myself, 'You have plenty of grain laid up for many years. Take life easy; eat, drink and be merry.'
> But God said to him, 'You fool! This very night your life will be demanded from you. Then who will get what you have prepared for yourself?'
> (vv. 18–21)

Jesus concluded as follows: 'This is how it will be with anyone who stores things up for himself but is not rich towards God' (v. 21 NIV 1984).

The goal of maximum satisfaction of human material wants is both foolish and wrong. We must be fully aware of the stark contrasts between, on the one hand, the biblical vision for work and economic life, and, on the other hand, that of today's prevailing mindset. That mindset has penetrated deeply into the ways in which many people today view work.

Conscious of that mindset, let us now dig deeper into how the biblical material applies to justice and the workplace.

Doing justice in the workplace: biblical teaching

There are some vital principles for us in the apostle Paul's letters to the Ephesians and the Colossians. These letters have parallels, so it is helpful to consider them together.

In both letters Paul first reminds his readers about the 'good news' (gospel), 'the word of truth' (Eph. 1:13; Col. 1:6); that is, the good news concerning the Lord Jesus Christ. Paul reminds his readers that they have come to believe this good news, the gospel of their salvation (Eph. 1:13). He then expounds key aspects of the message of Jesus Christ and of God's great plan and promises. This includes the wonderful new creation that I mentioned earlier: God's promise 'to bring unity to all things in heaven and on earth under Christ' (Eph. 1:10).[6]

In the second half of each letter Paul moves on to teach some of the implications of this message, and how it is to be applied in practical living. In both letters, as part of this practical application, the apostle addresses what we could call *relationships in the workplace*.

So for Christians, behaviour flows from belief. We cannot be saved *by* good deeds – only by grace, through faith in Christ and in what he has done for us by his death on the cross. But we are saved *in order to do* good deeds (Eph. 2:4–10). And part of the wonderful transforming work of God is that Christian believers have died to the old self, the former sinful way of life, and now have a *new self*: they are a new creation (2 Cor. 5:17). In Ephesians 4:22–24 Paul describes this new self in this way:[7]

> You were taught, with regard to your former way of life, to put off your old self, which is being corrupted by its deceitful desires; to be made new in the attitude of your minds; and to put on the new self, created to be like God in true righteousness and holiness.

Do you see what God says about this new self? It is created to be like him in 'true righteousness and holiness'. The word translated as 'righteousness' is the same word that we have seen previously (*dikaiosynē*). It includes, as we have seen, the idea of *justice*. So this righteousness-justice and holiness are to be worked out in all that we say and do. And that includes our behaviour in the workplace.

Radical principles

Here is what the letter to the Colossians says about relationships in the workplace:[8]

> Bondservants, obey in everything those who are your earthly masters, not by way of eye-service, as people-pleasers, but with sincerity of heart, fearing the Lord. Whatever you do, work heartily, as for the Lord and not for men, knowing that from the Lord you will receive the inheritance as your reward. You are serving the Lord Christ. For the wrongdoer will be paid back for the wrong he has done, and there is no partiality.
>
> Masters, treat your bondservants justly and fairly, knowing that you also have a Master in heaven.
>
> (Col. 3:22 – 4:1 ESVUK)

There are some vital principles for us here: including the requirement to work 'with all your heart' (v. 23 NIV 2011), and the command to those in power to treat 'justly and fairly' those who are under them.[9] These are radical principles, as we will see.

Obviously the cultural context of this letter is very different from our context today. For example, not many employees today refer to their boss as 'Master'! I will comment briefly, in a moment, about what a 'bondservant' was, and on questions about slave ownership. But the *principles* and *norms* here are of immense importance for us in our day.

Note that Paul clearly speaks to both sets of people at the same time: bondservants and masters (the equivalent in our day of employees and managers). The *relationships* between them are a central part of their Christian living. Bondservants have a responsibility *in the Lord* towards those they work for; and masters have a responsibility under the rule of *their* Master towards those under them. So this passage is all about relationships.

In both Colossians and Ephesians the teaching about workplace relationships is the third of three short sections (Col. 3:18 – 4:1; Eph. 5:22 – 6:9); and in both letters all of these three sections are about relationships and responsibilities – wives and husbands, children and parents, and bondservants and masters/owners. For every pair of relationships, both sets of commands must be taken together – the first must never be interpreted apart from the second.[10]

In the first century context all three pairs of relationships would typically have been lived out under the same roof (literally): the *household* was the place where many people both lived and worked.[11] In all three sections Paul repeatedly emphasizes that all of these relationships are to be lived out *in the Lord* and *for the Lord* (e.g. Col. 3:18, 22; Eph. 6:1): this is life under the rule of Christ; this is the new life of the kingdom.

The key principles for workplace relationships, in our passage from Colossians, are that bondservants must work with all their heart, and that masters (owners) must treat those under them *justly*. These are radical principles – both then and now.

The command to bondservants to work with all their heart (as serving the Lord) would be especially radical given the terribly hard conditions faced by many bondservants. The word translated in the ESVUK as 'bondservant' – *doulos* in the Greek – is often translated as 'slave'. A key feature of bondservants/slaves was that they had no freedom to escape. If they tried to escape, they could face death. This situation is very hard for us in the twenty-first century to imagine. Conditions for slaves/bondservants in the first century, in the Roman Empire and elsewhere, were gradually improving;[12] and some owners did emancipate (release) their bondservants; nevertheless, the basic condition of being bonded was one that none of us today would ever want to be in. Yet the biblical teaching is that all of these bondservants should work hard, as serving *the Lord* and not their human owners. This is radical.

A brief digression is needed at this point. You may well wonder why the apostle Paul did not say more to attack the institution of slavery. Much has been written about this question, but it is obviously not the focus of this book. What we can note, however, is that, taking the New Testament as a whole, much that is written there served gradually to undermine the institution of slavery. In this very letter to the Colossians, just a few verses earlier, Paul writes as follows about the new realm or new humanity God has brought into being in Christ: 'Here there is no Gentile or Jew, circumcised or uncircumcised, barbarian, Scythian, slave or free, but Christ is all, and is in all' (Col. 3:11).

This wonderful statement had, among other things, the effect of placing an explosive device under the dominant social distinctions and practices of the day. In Christ the social distinction (inequality) between slave and free has been abolished. We see exactly the same principle in Galatians 3:26–28. Something of the explosive impact of this new humanity is seen in how the apostle Paul writes to Philemon about his slave Onesimus.[13]

After that digression about what the New Testament says about the institution of slavery, we must come back to the radical principle that bondservants are to work with all their heart ('heartily', as the ESVUK says in Col. 3:23). Their relationship to their owners – the equivalent of 'bosses', in our terms – is to be governed by their relationship with the Lord Jesus Christ. They are to *obey* their earthly masters (v. 22), and this is out of reverence (godly fear) for the *Lord*.[14]

But before exploring further what this will mean in our context, we must also look at the responsibilities on the other side of the relationship: what is required of the masters ('bosses')? As I said earlier, we must consider both aspects of this workplace relationship. And the command to the 'earthly masters' is, if anything, even more radical: they must treat their bondservants 'justly and fairly'. It would have been very easy – and very tempting – for masters to treat their bondservants oppressively, harshly, unjustly. After all, the bondservants/slaves had no rights in law; they had no trade union to support them; they had no option to walk away. Why should not the owners (masters) force the bondservants to work as many hours as possible, with minimal pay and provision? Why bother treating them any differently from the practices of all the other owners/masters?

Paul gives one simple but powerful reason for why masters should treat those under them justly: 'knowing that you also have a Master in heaven' (Col. 4:1).[15] This heavenly Master and Lord is himself always just, and the earthly masters will have to give account to him. A performance review is generally a good motivator for any manager or employee. But here Paul reminds masters of the ultimate 'performance review' – judgment – that Christ will conduct of them at the end of this age. How much bigger a motivation is that! They are under the lordship of *Christ*.

Note that this same motivation is given both to bondservants and owners: the slaves are serving 'the Lord Christ' (3:24), and the masters 'also [like the bondservants] have a Master in heaven' (4:1). So the relationship of owners/masters to those under them is to be governed by their relationship to the Lord Jesus Christ. This is the same rule as it is for the bondservants – as we saw just now.

Can you imagine a Roman household in which the owner and bondservants have all become disciples of Jesus Christ? Can you picture what their day-to-day lives would be like if they were all living out what the New Testament teaches here? What harmony there would be – all working together for one heavenly Lord. The bondservants working from the heart, and the owner treating them justly. This would be a radical and practical demonstration of the kingdom of God, the saving rule of the Lord Jesus Christ.

What about households where not everyone has become a believer in Christ? Well, there may not be the same level of harmony. We all know it is harder to work with or under someone who is not being transformed by the love and goodness of Christ. But the same radical commands still apply.

Applying these radical principles in our workplace relationships

How does all of this apply to us today? Let us begin with those who have responsibilities as managers: the key principle is to treat the people who work for you (or under you) *justly*. If you are a manager, this is something God requires of you. Is that your prime commitment as a manager?

This principle is potent as well as radical. If Christians in management were to have this principle at the heart of their management, it would have a very powerful impact. For this is *not* a principle given much emphasis in most companies and organizations.

Christian managers have a tremendous opportunity, as well as a fundamental obligation, to do justice in the workplace – especially in how they treat the people who work for them. Here is an opportunity to shine distinctively as the light of the world.

What will it look like, in practice, to treat employees justly? There are at least four areas in which this principle should be applied: personal behaviour, wages and salaries, conditions of work, and helping colleagues to develop – which includes empowering the weak. Let us look at each of these in turn.

1 Personal behaviour

I have been emphasizing all along that a key aspect of doing economic justice involves the quality of relationships. So the behaviour of a manager, in relation to the people who work for him or her, is central to doing justice. The emphasis in Colossians 4:1 on treating people justly helps to bring this home even more. Clearly, different managers have different personalities, and different organizations may encourage different management styles; but how a Christian manager treats people at a one-to-one level is not negotiable. To treat people in a way that pleases God, to behave towards them in a godly way, is what we are commanded to do.

So suppose you are a manager and the company you work for has very strict rules on all sorts of aspects of how employees are to operate, how decisions are made, which forms must be filled in and when, and so on. You have to work within these constraints. You may think it better if a slightly more 'relaxed' way of operating were introduced, but, for the moment at least, that is not in your power to change. What you must do is treat people justly at a one-to-one level. (That may mean, for example, explaining carefully to someone in your team why certain things in that organization are done in a particular way.) You can still manage people justly whatever frustrations you may have about the 'company management style'. That is the central point.

Or suppose you are a manager and work for a charitable organization that has a very laid-back internal culture. Here you may prefer it if there were a *greater* degree of institutional discipline. Again, however, you have to work within the constraints around you. But, in your one-to-one relationships with your staff you must still treat people justly.

Whatever the context in which you manage, there may be times when you see people in your staff team being treated *unjustly* by others. Here it will be important to face the challenge of what it will mean, in that situation, to treat your staff justly. This may mean some kind of disagreement, even conflict, with others. Will you seek God's wisdom and grace about how to act for him in that context?

If you treat your team justly, I expect they will be aware that, as part of this, you are willing to defend them. That does not mean you turn a blind eye if they behave badly. Treating people justly does not mean tolerating poor performance. Indeed, part of justice is that people are held to account for poor behaviour. Even in that eventuality, however, your one-to-one relationship with such a colleague should be characterized by justice and fairness, not harshness or oppression.

2 Wages and salaries

In life, managers may or may not have any discretion over the wages and salaries paid to people in their team. So application of 'justice and fairness' to this dimension of workplace relationships will vary enormously from situation to situation. But there are still some key points for us to be aware of. First, think back to what I said, in the introduction to this chapter, about the way in which lots of people view their work. In surveys 45–49% of people in the UK agree with the statement 'A job is just a way of earning money.' So if you are a manager, you must take account of this – it is part of the context. For a lot of people in your team, the money they earn is not only important to them in their job: it is the only important thing about their job. It follows that this could easily become an area where they might feel aggrieved; that is, if the amount they are paid is perceived by them to be *unjustly* low, then the level of their commitment to their work role could rapidly tail off. So you must be alert and sensitive in this area.

A second key point follows in part from the first: if you are a manager, then part of treating your team members justly is that you do this with such clarity and consistency that they know you are supporting them when it comes to their wage/salary. As I said earlier, you may or may not have much discretion over wage policy. But what you can do is play your part in standing up, within the organization, for what is just in relation to your team members – especially regarding wages and salaries.

Third, the way that companies and other organizations approach wages and salaries can be a barometer of how they regard the people they employ, and managers must be conscious of this. In particular, organizations can have two highly opposed attitudes towards their employees: some see employees as their most important *asset*; others, by contrast, view employees essentially as a *cost*. The latter is endorsed by, strangely enough, a large number of both economists and accountants. (These two groups do not always agree with each other!) In mainstream economic analysis the wage paid to workers (to 'labour') is often viewed as essentially a cost of production. Indeed, although labour is recognized as a necessary part of what goes into producing goods and services, a 'factor of production' in economics textbook language, the main category applied to workers is that of 'cost'. It follows that economic analysis assumes that firms will seek to minimize all costs, which means paying as little as possible.

As for accountants, well, they often take on the role of keeping down costs as much as possible; and so, again, wages and salaries can be viewed as costs to be minimized. (Hence the perhaps surprising agreement between two professions often seen as being at odds with one another!)

An alternative approach, however, is to view employees as an *asset*; indeed, the most important asset for an organization. Below are a couple of quotations in support of that approach. First, 'Employees are a company's most important asset. They are the face of the company and directly impact customer experience and satisfaction. However, few organizations listen to their employees as part of a strategic initiative.'[16] That last observation should be of deep concern to managers and leaders who are followers of Christ: to *listen to* others is a crucial part of loving and respecting them.

And here, second, is a highly experienced leadership consultant and executive coach, Rodger Dean Duncan, in a blog entitled 'Nine Ways to Keep Your Company's Most Valuable Asset – Its Employees': 'Successful organizations lead the *whole* person, acknowledging that employees have heads and hearts.'[17] Indeed, with *this* view of employees, the fact that about half of people see their job as 'just a way of earning money' is challenged. I do not mean that the fact is denied. Rather, the assumption that it has to stay that way is challenged. Duncan argues:

> Employees don't want to be regarded as mere 'stomachs.' They can't be motivated only with salary and benefits. In today's environment, the old notion of 'just be grateful you have a job' is a fast ticket to low performance and high turnover . . . Many studies on [employee] retention agree on what influences employees to stay: meaningful, challenging work . . . a chance to grow and learn . . . a good work environment . . . recognition and respect.[18]

This approach seems to me much closer to a biblical understanding of human beings and how we should be treated, compared to the previous approach.

3 Conditions of work

The quotations above take us directly into (more briefly) a third area of application of the principle of treating employees justly; that is, the broader set of conditions in which people work. As Duncan argued, employees will typically be encouraged by a good work environment, and by recognition and respect. These things are also, I would argue, central to the Bible's principle of treating workers justly. As the Lord Jesus taught, in what has become known as the 'Golden Rule', 'in everything, do to others what you would have them do to you, for this sums up the Law and the Prophets'

(Matt. 7:12). This is all part of the new-creation righteousness that God is working in all those who follow Christ.

So if you are a manager, how can you help to promote good conditions of work for your team, department or organization? This book is not a 'how to' manual of management, but here are a couple of points that can help to encourage constructive thinking and appropriate action. First, the *physical environment* in which people work is important, and part of good management is to give attention to this. People are the key asset, remember. We in the West can be thankful to God that there is, in the twenty-first century, a widespread understanding and appreciation of what a good physical environment for work should be like; for example, a suitable temperature, ergonomically appropriate office environments, and good health and safety standards.

We can all appreciate that health and safety regulations have the potential to be overdone and be excessively bureaucratic, but their core concern is thoroughly biblical and a right reflection of a desire for fair treatment of fellow human beings. There is a striking verse in Deuteronomy 22 that gives an important indication of God's mind and heart regarding such matters (Deut. 22:8): 'When you build a new house, make a parapet around your roof so that you may not bring the guilt of bloodshed on your house if someone falls from the roof.'

Clearly, the context is of a flat roof, not gabled. In the Middle East it was and is common for the (flat) roof of a house to be a space where people can go – to sit and enjoy the sunset, and so on. The meaning of the verse in Deuteronomy is clear enough: someone who builds a house should include suitable precautions to help ensure that people who go up onto the roof cannot easily fall off. And such precautions will help ensure that the builder and his household are spared the moral guilt that will come upon them if they fail to take those precautions. It is a short and simple verse, but with profound implications for just treatment of fellow human beings with regard to safety precautions.

Another dimension of good working conditions concerns the hours people work, length of rest breaks, holiday provision and other time-related aspects. Again, the principle is that people are a key asset, and should be treated fairly. It is clear, of course, that managers must operate within the constraints of the organization or company. But, as we saw earlier, managers who act justly will act consistently in support of their team, whatever those constraints.

It can also be a useful 'thought experiment' to ponder on what *oppressive* or *unjust* working conditions may look like, and then to try to ensure that people in your team are *not* treated like that. For example, are staff in principle allowed adequate time for breaks during the day (or night)? Clearly, there can sometimes be emergencies and urgent deadlines – but having breaks is vital to good functioning as a human being.

4 Helping colleagues to develop

Quite a lot of employers give emphasis, rightly, to 'professional development' for employees. This makes sense from a number of perspectives; for example, given that people are a key asset for an organization, it is only sensible to develop those staff/assets – to get the most out of them, as it were. Also, key employees may simply leave and go elsewhere if their own professional and personal development is not encouraged. Here is Rodger Dean Duncan again:

> Many studies on retention agree on what influences employees to stay: meaningful, challenging work . . . a chance to grow and learn . . . a good work environment . . . recognition and respect. Notice how many of these fall under the umbrella of 'psychological ownership.'[19]

But does Christian/biblical thinking have anything to add to these important 'common sense' guidelines? If we recall that biblical economic justice means treating people appropriately, according to the norms and principles given by God, then we will want to look carefully at Scripture to discover what insights it provides on these matters. And a central principle here – as we have seen already in this chapter – is the 'Golden Rule' taught by the Lord Jesus: 'in everything, do to others what you would have them do to you' (Matt. 7:12).

Think for a few moments about people who helped *you* to develop. Where would you be without the input, teaching, training and support they gave you? Then, if you are a manager or leader, apply the Golden Rule to your attitude to people in your team or organization. How can you help them to develop? To find answers to that kind of question, and to put those answers into practice, is a requirement of treating people appropriately – a requirement of economic justice.

This kind of thinking and action, then, is mandatory for any follower of Christ who has responsibilities in managing people. It is not simply yet another item on a list of things to be attended to, if and when you have time. Still less is it a matter of paying only lip service to professional development.

But there is another crucial dimension to this. Recall that a biblical understanding of economic justice includes an emphasis on how *people who are poor and needy* within a community (or society) are treated. We must always have an eye open for those who are needy and weak. So suppose you are a manager and your team includes someone you know is struggling (needy), and/or is poor. What might it mean for you to support this person? In what ways can you help to give him or her 'a hand up'? How can you empower?

In a setting where 'the survival of the fittest' reigned, such questions would of course be ludicrous. But biblical thinking and action cannot give encouragement or succour to such a setting. Quite the opposite. In Leviticus 19, for example, God tells Moses to give the following commands to the people of Israel:

> When a foreigner resides among you in your land, do not ill-treat them. The foreigner residing among you must be treated as your native-born. Love them as yourself, for you were foreigners in Egypt. I am the LORD your God.
> (vv. 33–34)

Foreigners would be in a very weak position, socially and economically. But that is no reason to take advantage of them. Instead, the Israelites were to recall their own extremely vulnerable plight when they and their ancestors were in Egypt, as foreigners and slaves. As the Lord had compassion on them, so they should have compassion for the needy and vulnerable around them. And so they were commanded to love the foreigners as they loved themselves. The same principle applies to how we are to treat those in our organization who are weak and struggling. How can I help to equip this person to overcome challenges and to grow?

5 Employees: work with all your heart – you are serving the Lord Christ

Having spent some time considering the responsibilities on the side of the manager, let us now look at the people on the other side of these workplace relationships: employees. Although my coverage of this will be briefer, the challenges are just as radical.

We all breathe the cultural air around us. That is unavoidable. In twenty-first-century Western society the dominant culture around paid work – as we saw earlier – is that work is primarily about *me*. Recall that almost half of people in Britain (in surveys) agree with the statement 'A job is just a way of earning money.' In addition, for many people work is about meeting *my* needs, attaining *my* goals, fulfilling *my* career plan and earning money for *my* leisure time. This is the prevailing culture. And, since we live and breathe this culture, it is very hard not to be influenced by it. For example, if you are employed in an office where *grumbling* about work is part of the dominant conversation pattern and culture, it is pretty hard not to end up joining in!

But that is precisely why the teaching of the New Testament about work is so important. The teaching in Colossians 3 – that we should work with all our heart, and that in our work we are serving the Lord Christ – is radically opposed to today's prevailing culture. That is very challenging. And the importance of the teaching is that it can help us deal with that challenge. How do we resist being influenced by the prevailing culture regarding work? By reading God's word, meditating on it, taking it in and seeking the empowering of the

Holy Spirit to *obey* God's word, more and more, from Monday through to Sunday.

Followers of Christ are called by him to be part of his counter-culture. So we must resist the influence of all aspects of the dominant culture that go against the will of God. Part of this resistance is to identify the prevailing culture, and especially those parts of it that fall short of God's standards. So if you are in employment, pray for discernment as you reflect on what the cultural air is around you. And pray for the Lord to help you think and behave differently.

If, for example, the cultural norm is to grumble about work and various aspects of the job situation, recognize that; and then find out what attitudes will, by contrast, *please* the Lord. Remember: if Christian believers who were bondservants in the Roman Empire could work heartily and do all for the glory of God, then surely you can too?

In view of today's prevailing culture it is also important to take on board another key feature of what Colossians 3:23–25 say about work, namely the *motivation* of serving the Lord Christ. The vital truth here is about the judgment we will each face, when the Lord comes again. This Lord whom we are serving will come again to judge the living and the dead. So each of us will have to give an account of our own service, including service in the workplace. That should be a powerful motivation for us. As I said earlier, this is the ultimate performance review.

Please remember this, however: if our faith for our eternal salvation is *in Christ alone* and in what he has done for us on the cross, then nothing about the judgment to come can deny our salvation. Salvation is by grace alone, through faith alone.

Conclusion

As our reflections on the New Testament teaching about doing justice in the workplace come to a close, it is important to recall the emphasis in that teaching on relationships in the workplace. If you are someone with managerial responsibilities, how much easier your life would be if at least some of those people were putting into practice the Bible's radical teaching to employees. And, similarly, if you are employed, how much better your work would be if your boss were a follower of Christ who treats you justly.

Now I am writing this at a time when the percentage of people in Britain who are committed Christians is very small – in single figures. So a scenario where there is both a Christian manager and Christian employees will of course be highly unusual. But it is still well worth imagining what it would be like, in our day, to be part of that kind of scenario. For that can help to spur us to serve the Lord better, and to work harder at treating people justly.

4

Church communities: beacons of economic justice

Jesus said to his disciples:

> A new commandment I give to you, that you love one another: just as I have loved you, you also are to love one another. By this all people will know that you are my disciples, if you have love for one another.
> (John 13:34–35 ESVUK)

The apostle Paul wrote to the Christians in Galatia, 'Therefore, as we have opportunity, let us do good to all people, especially to those who belong to the family of believers' (Gal. 6:10). Jesus said to his disciples:

> You are the light of the world. A city set on a hill cannot be hidden. Nor do people light a lamp and put it under a basket, but on a stand, and it gives light to all in the house. In the same way, let your light shine before others, so that they may see your good works and give glory to your Father who is in heaven.
> (Matt. 5:14–16 ESVUK)

Introduction

Beacons shine brightly – especially when things are dark. Jesus Christ declares to his followers – probably to their amazement – that *they* are the light of the world. They are to shine brightly. If you, today, are a follower of Jesus Christ, then you, with your church community, are also to shine brightly like a beacon. And a big part of shining brightly, says Jesus Christ, is by doing good works.

What has this to do with economic justice? A lot! Back in chapter 1 we saw that one of the key aspects of biblical economic justice is treating justly those who are poor and needy within a community, on always having an eye open for the poor and needy. So to do justice in relation to those who are in need is part of the 'doing good' to which Jesus Christ calls his church.

A lovely example of this is a woman named Tabitha, who is mentioned in Acts 9: she was one of the first followers of Jesus Christ, and 'was always doing good and helping the poor' (9:36). She understood that part of the heart of God is helping the poor.[1]

Now some of you may be thinking, 'In my view, economic justice is about campaigning for changes to unjust structures; one-to-one help for the poor is about charity, not justice.' In that case let me gently suggest you go back to chapter 1 and read what I tried to show there. The whole argument of this book is that a *biblical* understanding of economic justice is about treating people appropriately, according to the principles and norms given by God: and this justice *includes* how we treat people – not least the poor and needy – at a personal, one-to-one level. If we are followers of Christ, then we must be willing to let *our* ideas be reshaped in the light of *his* teaching. For example, as we saw in chapter 1, Job was a 'father to the needy' (Job 29:16). God's own justice includes how he treats those in need (e.g. Pss 143:1; 145:17), and we should do likewise.

The goal of this chapter is to show how *church communities* must support those who are poor and needy – especially those *within* the church community who are poor. This emphasis reflects the first two of the New Testament verses quoted at the head of this chapter: Jesus Christ taught plainly the importance of followers of Christ loving *one another*, and the powerful way in which such love will speak to all people, including those who are outside the church community; and the apostle Paul exhorted Christians to 'do good to all people, especially those who belong to the family of believers' (Gal. 6:10). But this is never an 'exclusive club' kind of love, and so of course we are to do good to all people. As we learn more and more to support the poor and needy, our church communities will become ever brighter beacons of economic justice.[2]

What would such support for the poor and needy look like in our churches in the twenty-first century? What are the biblical principles to guide us here? How can we do more of this aspect of economic justice in practice? How can the help given by church communities here *complement* the support that is offered by official government structures (the 'welfare state')? And what is the relationship between doing economic justice and the church's central calling to proclaim *in words* the good news of Jesus Christ, which people so desperately need to hear? Can these really go hand in hand? What does it mean in practice to 'do justice and preach grace'?

These are the questions this chapter seeks to answer.

Biblical principles for how to support those who are poor and needy

In the Old Testament God gave the people of Israel a package of provisions for how they should treat people who were poor and needy.[3] As we read and study this material given in the word of God, we learn more about the mind of God – especially in relation to the poor and needy. And God's mind does not change. So this material is vital for us today.

As we look at the Old Testament teaching, I am going to highlight two interrelated principles for the people of God; and I will also show how these principles underpin what the New Testament teaches.[4] First, it is essential that the material needs of everybody in a community are provided for, and therefore compassionate provision for the poor and needy is commanded.[5] Second, there is a strong emphasis on enabling the poor and needy, wherever possible, to earn a living. These two principles are interrelated.

The first principle is demonstrated in the Old Testament in many ways: there is a whole range of provisions to ensure that the needs of the poor are met. For example, as discussed in chapter 1 above, every third year a tenth of the produce of any piece of land was to be given to those who had no land – the Levites, resident foreigners and widows (see Deut. 14:22–29) – with the intention that all of these people 'may come and eat and be satisfied' (v. 29; restated in Deut. 26:12).[6] This provision would enable people to store the tithe, and then prepare food, over a substantial period of time. Also, Israelites were strongly exhorted to be open-handed, by lending to anyone in need at any time:

> If anyone is poor among your fellow Israelites in any of the towns of the land that the LORD your God is giving you, do not be hard-hearted or tight-fisted towards them. Rather, be open-handed and freely lend them whatever they need … Give generously to them and do so without a grudging heart …
> (Deut. 15:7–8, 10)

In addition, at harvest time there was provision for the poor and the sojourners or resident foreigners to share in the harvest:

> When you reap the harvest of your land, do not reap to the very edges of your field or gather the gleanings of your harvest. Leave them for the poor and for the foreigner residing among you. I am the LORD your God.
> (Lev. 23:22)[7]

The second principle mandates ways of enabling the poor and needy, wherever possible, to earn a living. This is seen most clearly in Leviticus 25. This chapter is well known for requiring that in the fiftieth ('Jubilee') year all were to return to their family property (land) and their own clan (wider family group) – even if their weak economic circumstances had forced them to sell their land and move elsewhere during those fifty years.[8] But this chapter also sets out a range of ways in which *during* those intervening fifty years people who became poor were to be supported, in such a way that they might earn a living and 'continue to live among you' (Lev. 25:36). So, for example, in verses 25–27:

> If one of your fellow Israelites becomes poor and sells some of their property, their nearest relative is to come and redeem what they have sold. If, however, there is no one to redeem it for them but later on they prosper and acquire sufficient means to redeem it themselves, they are to determine the value for the years since they sold it and refund the balance to the one to whom they sold it; they can then go back to their own property.

Let me remind you that the setting was an agricultural economy: most people earned a living from the land, and that is how they provided for themselves and their household. (We will consider a little later how the principle here can be applied in a twenty-first-century economy that is primarily *not* agricultural.) So to be back in control of your own property was of much greater significance than, say, buying a piece of property in our contemporary context. In Old Testament times being back at your own property/land meant that you would earn your livelihood there. So verses 25–27 set out two of the ways in which someone who had become poor could be helped back to earn a living on their own piece of land: a near relative – a 'kinsman redeemer', such as Boaz in the book of Ruth – could buy it back on their behalf; or the people themselves, if they had prospered elsewhere, could redeem it for themselves.[9]

Did you note that the role of the wider community here is crucial? The person in poverty would be helped by a near relative: someone from the wider family. And the whole community had to accept all of this teaching; for example, the person who had initially purchased the land from the impoverished person was *mandated* to sell it back, at a suitable price (v. 27). So in case you are wondering what all of this has to do with *church* communities in the twenty-first century, the answer is 'a great deal!' The New Testament teaches that the people of God now comprises followers of Jesus Christ, and the *principles* from the Old Testament apply to church communities now as much as they did to the Israelite community in Old Testament times.

Another provision in Leviticus 25 for someone who became poor is given in verses 35–37:

If any of your fellow Israelites become poor and are unable to support themselves among you, help them as you would a foreigner and stranger, so that they can continue to live among you. Do not take interest or any profit from them, but fear your God, so that they may continue to live among you. You must not lend them money at interest or sell them food at a profit.

In these verses the focus is on helping such a person by means of a loan, at zero interest. In my chapter here we have already seen, a few paragraphs above, this kind of assistance prescribed in Deuteronomy 15. Now this *loan*-based assistance for the poor may seem strange to our ears in the West. However, in recent years many people in the Global South have benefited from 'microfinance': small loans, at low rates of interest, designed to give them 'a hand up'.[10] So this kind of provision is far from being irrelevant to today's world. In Old Testament times the way that zero-interest loans functioned would be this: people who had fallen on hard times would, with the support of the loan, be able to buy some seed, and/ or other resource, that would enable them to resume earning a living – to 'prosper', as Leviticus 25:26 puts it. Once they had prospered sufficiently, they would repay the loan.[11]

Again, we should be thinking creatively about how a church community in the twenty-first century can apply the principle here: how to help someone get back to providing *by their own work* for themselves and their household. A later section in this chapter focuses on how churches today can apply these important principles taught in the Old Testament.

Going back to Leviticus 25, a third provision for someone who becomes poor is that they should be permitted to live *and work* in someone else's household (vv. 39–43). The formal route here was that impoverished people would 'sell' themselves to someone else (v. 39); however, the biblical text immediately states that they are to be well treated – *not* 'as slaves' but in the same way that a hired worker or temporary resident would be treated (v. 40). So this person – probably along with immediate family – would have both the dignity of doing work and the security of being part of this other household. Verse 43 concludes the paragraph, 'Do not rule over them ruthlessly, but fear your God.'

So, in all this teaching we see the principle that people who became poor were to be enabled to get back to a position where they could, through their own work, gain a livelihood for themselves and their household: the principle is that they might continue to live 'among you' (vv. 35–36, 40).

'There should be no poor . . . there will always be poor people . . .' (Deut. 15:4, 11 NIV 1984)

Let me take you on a short but important digression here. In the above subheading the two phrases in Deuteronomy 15 – a section I have already referred to in this chapter more than once – may seem to contradict one another. But, taken together, they provide a tension that is as important for us today as it was in Old Testament times. On the one hand, the clear *purpose* set by God for the people of Israel was that 'there should be no poor among you' (Deut. 15:4 NIV 1984); on the other hand, the reality was that there would always be poor in the land.

It is important to see that this clear purpose – 'no poor among you' – was part of God's desire to *bless* his people and was linked to their obedience to him; so we must note how the whole sentence (vv. 4–6) reads. The previous verse states that the Israelites might require payment of a loan made to a foreigner. But they had to cancel, in the seventh year, any debt owed by a fellow Israelite – a loan that would have been made in the first place because someone had become poor, as we have seen from Leviticus 25. Verses 4–6 continue:

> However, there should be no poor among you, for in the land the LORD your God is giving you to possess as your inherit-ance, he will richly bless you, if only you fully obey the LORD

your God and are careful to follow all these commands I am giving you today. For the LORD your God will bless you as he has promised . . .
(NIV 1984)[12]

God's clear desire was that there should be no poor people in the land, but the attainment of this goal was linked closely with full obedience by the whole Israelite community. In other words, a barometer of a faithful community of God's people would be the absence of poverty. Incidentally, recognition of this purpose is an important corrective for anyone inclined to think that material poverty is part of God's original intention for humankind.

That clear goal – 'no poor among you' – has to be balanced, however, against the realism of verses 7–11 in that same chapter: so verse 7 begins, 'If anyone is poor among your fellow Israelites . . .'; the command is then given (v. 8) to lend freely whatever that person needs; and then verse 11 concludes the section, 'There will always be poor people in the land. Therefore I command you to be open-handed towards your fellow Israelites who are poor and needy in your land.'

We must, then, recognize this tension between God's clear desire ('no poor among you') and the realities of a fallen, sinful world (there 'will always be poor people in the land'). To strive for the best, while being conscious that we will not fully arrive there in this age, is an important combination.[13]

It is striking that in the New Testament both aspects of this tension regarding the poor are stated plainly. So, on the one hand, Luke wrote of the early church community in Jerusalem, there 'was no needy person among them' (Acts 4:34). On the other hand, Jesus Christ himself said, in the context of his being anointed with expensive perfume by Mary at Bethany, 'You will always have the poor among you, but you will not always have me' (John 12:8).[14] Biblical commentators and scholars widely acknowledge that both of these statements are deliberate references to Deuteronomy 15. We will return shortly to how church communities in the New Testament sought to support the poor and needy.

After that important digression, let me sum up this section as a whole. We have been looking at two interrelated principles demonstrated in the Old Testament. First, the material needs of everybody in a community must be provided for; therefore compassionate provision for the poor and needy was commanded. Second, people who became poor were to be enabled to get back, wherever possible, to a position where, through their own work, they could gain a livelihood for themselves and their household.

But we must take on board that the two principles are intertwined; for example, the *way in which* people who were poor and needy should be helped would often involve their getting back to earning a living for themselves and their households. The role of gleaning illustrates this: what was offered was a way of people sharing in the harvest by their own efforts. Similarly, compassionate zero-interest loans would function precisely by enabling people to re-engage with earning their own living.

Some people, such as the infirm, would be unable to provide for themselves. For them other provisions, such as the third-year tithe, would help to provide support, and in any case they would be cared for as members of a household.

Having seen those two important and interconnected principles, let us now turn to the New Testament and the way in which church communities applied them.

New Testament churches and support for the poor and needy

The first of those two principles – the obligation to provide for the poor and needy within the community – was implemented by New Testament churches in a number of ways. Right from the start the church community in Jerusalem 'sold property and possessions to give to anyone who had need' (Acts 2:45). In Acts 4:34 we read that 'there was no needy person among them'; as noted earlier, this is a reference to the poverty-free goal that God set for his people back in Deuteronomy 15. Acts 4:34–35 explains how this outcome was achieved:

there was no needy person among them. For from time to time those who owned land or houses sold them, brought the money from the sales and put it at the apostles' feet, and it was distributed to anyone who had need.

The final clause in that passage shows that what happened was not that, by some magical or mysterious process, needs never arose; rather, material needs were met by distribution from a fund that was sourced by people 'from time to time' selling land or property.[15] This seems to be a straightforward application not only of the Old Testament teaching but also of Jesus Christ's command to his followers (Luke 12:33): 'Sell your possessions and give to the poor.'

Another way, a number of years later, in which the poor were to be helped was a one-off collection organized by the apostle Paul. This was to bring aid to Christian believers in Jerusalem, who by this time were suffering greatly from a famine.[16]

A further aspect of poverty-relief ministry was specifically for widows. (Under the Middle Eastern socio-economic arrangements of the first century, women whose husbands had died would often be particularly vulnerable in material terms.) An early example of this is in Acts 6:1–6, which refers to the 'daily distribution of food' to widows.[17] A few decades later we can see from Paul's first letter to Timothy – a church leader – that by then the provision of material support for widows included a formal listing of some kind (1 Tim. 5:3–10). However, it is important to notice from this letter of Paul that church leaders were conscious of issues such as how to blend the responsibility of the *church* community and the responsibility of natural (blood) *families* with regard to widows. In verses 3–4 Paul teaches, for example, as follows:

Give proper recognition to those widows who are really in need. But if a widow has children or grandchildren, these should learn first of all to put their religion into practice by caring for their own family and so repaying their parents and grandparents, for this is pleasing to God.

This is a highly significant way of seeing how the poverty-relief ministry of *church communities* can work *alongside* what is provided in the wider society. That same approach can surely be applied in our contemporary world. (I return to this point later in the chapter.)

Bruce Winter helpfully explains some of the economic and cultural Graeco-Roman context here, and especially the practice of the marriage *dowry*:

> The dowry, which was provided by the bride's father always accompanied a woman to her marriage. It constituted an important legal aspect of marriage ... In the event of a husband's death, the laws governing the dowry were clearly defined. A widow was cared for by the person in charge of that dowry. Two options were open to her. If she had children, she might remain in the deceased husband's home. There she would be maintained by the new 'lord' [*kyrios* in Greek] of the household, possibly her son. She could also return to her parents, taking her dowry back to her family. The choice appears to have been hers.[18]

It is also notable from 1 Timothy 5 that expectations were laid upon the recipient widows, as well as on the donor church community (see v. 9).

So church communities from the earliest days took very seriously their obligations to support people in their material need.

In the New Testament we also see some ways in which the second principle from the Old Testament was applied; that is, the importance of people in need being 'helped up' to a position where they could again work to provide for themselves, for their household and indeed for others who were in need. An example of this is given by the apostle Paul himself in his own behaviour and work. In his farewell talk to the elders of the church at Ephesus, he includes the following:

> You yourselves know that these hands of mine have supplied my own needs and the needs of my companions. In everything

I did, I showed you that by this kind of hard work we must help the weak, remembering the words the Lord Jesus himself said: 'It is more blessed to give than to receive.'
(Acts 20:34–35)

In his letter to the Ephesians Paul teaches the same principle: 'Anyone who has been stealing must steal no longer, but must work, doing something useful with their own hands, that they may have something to share with those in need' (Eph. 4:28). In other words, someone who has previously been living a lifestyle *different* from that of supporting, through work, themselves and their family is now strongly exhorted to return to God's norms.

Rhodes, Holt and Fikkert argue that the same principle underlies what Paul writes in 2 Thessalonians 3:6–13:

what sometimes gets lost in translation when we read 2 Thessalonians 3:10 – 'If anyone is not willing to work, let him not eat' [ESVUK] – is that Paul was criticizing people who do not *want to work* (the Greek word translated 'willing' normally includes the idea of desiring). The idea isn't that people who can't find work should be allowed to starve but, rather, that people who do not desire to work ought not to be allowed to eat from the community's common table.[19]

The understanding here is that the church community had a regular practice of shared meals – which would on occasion include celebrating the Lord's Supper (Holy Communion) within that shared meal. As we have seen plenty of times in this book, there are responsibilities upon everyone in a community, and these are often reciprocal. Here the New Testament picture is that participation in meals comes with the responsibility to provide, if you are able to do so, for yourself and your household.

Another way of describing what is happening with all these practices is to bring in the notion of *dependency culture*. That is to say, the biblical teachings seem designed to *avoid* an unhealthy dependency culture – wherever possible, people should endeavour to provide for themselves and their household. This is part of the creation pattern going right back to Genesis 1 – 2. Life can deal tough experiences to people: but if we never get back to a healthy way of providing for ourselves and our household – and indeed to having something left for *others* in need, as the apostle Paul urged – then ultimately that is not good for us.

But the vision here is *not* one of individualistic independence; instead, it is of interdependence. We belong together as human beings, and as we go through life there are times when others are relatively more dependent on us, and times when we are more dependent on others. And all of this reminds us that we are *always* dependent on God, our loving and almighty Father, whose faithfulness is indeed great!

Applying these biblical principles in our church communities today

How can we apply these biblical patterns? How can our churches become brighter beacons of economic justice as we support those who are poor and needy? Here are some areas for us to think about, and some suggestions for the kinds of actions we should explore.[20]

Supporting the poor and needy in your church community

Here is a question. How does *your* church administer provision for the poor within your church family? You may not know the answer – in which case, it would be a good idea to find out!

Perhaps your church community does not organize any such provision – in which case, it is a biblical principle your church ought to start thinking about. We have seen the priority given in both the Old Testament and New Testament to helping the poor within God's community to ensure that all material needs are met.

Remember: we are talking here about meeting the immediate needs of people. The second biblical principle, as we have seen, is about helping people, wherever possible, to get to the point where they can support themselves and their household – we will come shortly to applications of this second principle. There are significant practical aspects for our church communities to bear in mind here, including the following:

1 *Sensitivity* to the people who are poor and needy: it may not be an easy thing for someone to admit that they are struggling in material terms. So, at least in a British context, it is very important to ensure confidentiality.[21] Therefore it is vital to ensure *both* that information about the provision offered by the church community is easily available, *and* that people seeking to take up this provision can do so in complete confidentiality.

2 *Do not let this be yet another burden for the pastor!* We should take our cue here from Acts 6: wherever possible the provision for the poor and needy should be administered by a group of suitably experienced and spiritually wise people. Perhaps the senior pastor/minister, if there is one, or the senior leadership, could be a first port of call for people who are in need, and then their situation can be quietly handed over to the administering team.

3 *Be aware of the second biblical principle*: the importance of helping people, wherever possible, to get to the point where they can support themselves and their household. This may mean that the administering team should have conversations with the person who is struggling materially, with a view to the way forward. Perhaps there is another group of people (see below) in the church community who are dedicated to giving people a 'hand up' in this way; if so, then the administering group may want to encourage the person in need to sit and talk with this second group, in due course. These are evidently delicate matters, which is why it is vital that those involved are experienced and spiritually wise.

4 *Have a 'giving a hand up' group.* It seems to me that it is better if this is a different group of people from the administering group – especially if the needs are quite considerable. The first group will have plenty of responsibilities on their hands simply to organize and administer the provision, and to handle the relationships sensitively. The role of the 'giving a hand up' group

is to support people in getting to the point where they can again provide for themselves and their household through paid work. This can involve things such as helping to arrange interviews at job centres (and offering lifts as needed), working with people to develop their CV, supporting people as they look for jobs (e.g. finding suitable websites, giving help as needed with Internet skills), and offering practice interviews.

Now I can imagine that some readers have been thinking along the lines of 'My church is in quite an affluent area, and I don't think we have anyone who is poor and needy.' There are various things to say in response. First, we must be aware that people may be in material need in *any* area, whether well-off or poor, but they may feel ashamed and so try to hide that need. Anyone can lose a job, whether in a rich or a poor area. Anyone can get into difficulties with debt, credit, a mortgage or with gambling. So we must not simply assume that no one in our church is in need; instead, our church communities should be sufficiently compassionate and sensitive that if anyone does fall upon hard times, they know that their church family will listen and offer support.

Therefore, second, it may be a good idea even for a church located in an affluent area to set up the kinds of groups I have suggested above – especially if the church is numerically large. The larger the group the more likely it is that some people in that group will fall into difficult circumstances.

Third, the New Testament offers wonderful examples of *church partnerships*: this includes partnerships whereby church communities who faced material hardship received help from other churches. The collection organized by the apostle Paul – mentioned earlier in this chapter – is a clear example. So imagine for a moment that a church in a more affluent area decided that it would like to help a church in a poorer area in the latter's support for their poor and needy. Is it feasible? How might it work? It seems to me that there is clear scope for developing partnerships along those lines. Perhaps the church in the better-off area could begin by simply sending some people to get to know better the people and the situation in the less well-off area; then people could sit down and begin to explore the possibilities.

The fact that, in Britain at least, there are well-established 'divides' between richer and poorer areas, *and between church communities along the same lines* is a negative feature of our church life. Would it not be more pleasing to God if we in our church communities and church partnerships were learning to cross these divides? The vision of the New Testament is of a church community in which all believers in Christ are *one*, regardless of social status or economic well-being. This is plain from passages such as Ephesians 2:11–22 and Galatians 3:26–28.

Of course, it is important to begin from where we are. If the socio-economic features of our church communities are somewhat homogeneous, then we must accept this as the starting point. But then, by God's grace, we must seek to develop from there. And one way to do that is to explore the potential for partnerships between churches from different locations and with different prevailing socio-economic features.

Doing good to the poor and needy in the wider community

The main focus of this chapter thus far has been on supporting the poor and needy within our church communities. This is partly because the New Testament devotes considerable emphasis to this, and because, I suspect, a fair number of churches at this time have not yet fully woken up to our obligations before God in this area. But the New Testament also teaches, as we have seen earlier, that followers of Christ are to do good to all – and this clearly includes a commitment to the poor and needy. So this is also part of our calling to be beacons of economic justice.

How are we to go about fulfilling this responsibility? Well, this is not rocket science! Once we have accepted that God calls all his people to have a special eye open for those who are poor and needy, then it is a matter, first of all, of looking around us – especially in the villages, towns and cities where we live – and finding out about who is struggling materially.

In the UK in recent years Christians have developed ministries – including church-based ministries – in two notable aspects where people struggle in material terms. One is food banks; the other is work with people who have debt problems.[22] But there are other dimensions of difficulty too: one is housing (including homelessness); another is fuel – many people who are poor struggle to pay the bills for heating and lighting in their homes; 'fuel poverty' is a great concern. As we learn to look around us – perhaps aided by conducting surveys, together with other research – we can seek wisdom from God in discerning where we might focus some effort.

In all the ways in which we seek to support those who are poor and needy – both within the church family and in the wider community – it is helpful to consider how churches can *complement* the provision that is offered by the state sector ('the welfare state') and by existing charities. We saw earlier how the New Testament provision for widows – see 1 Timothy 5 – worked alongside the social, cultural and economic patterns and institutions prevailing at that time in that part of the world. In the present-day UK, where monetary support through statutory authorities is available for those in need, it may not be sensible to seek to bolster those financial provisions with additional money, for this could end up to the detriment of the person in need if state support is withdrawn pound-for-pound for regular gifts of money received from elsewhere. But there are other ways in which people can be helped with their immediate needs: the examples of food banks and support with debt problems testify to what can be done.

Another key thing to bear in mind as we reach out to the poor and needy in the wider community is that *both* of the interconnected principles that we have seen in our exploration of the Bible are important. First, the material needs of everybody in a community must be provided for: practical and compassionate provision for the poor and needy is commanded. Second, people who become poor are to be supported to get back, wherever possible, to a position where they can gain a livelihood for themselves and their household – through their own work.

What might it mean to apply *both* of these principles as we seek to support the poor and needy in a wider community? Consider this example given, in the USA context, by Rhodes, Holt and Fikkert. It is a soup kitchen run by Episcopal Community Services (ECS) in Kansas City:

> Each day, homeless patrons eat alongside doctors, police officers, college kids and anybody else . . . it's all free . . . you get served by volunteer waitstaff who treat you like you're in a restaurant, which is what this unusual soup kitchen looks like . . .[23]

> ECS doesn't stop there. They recognise that homeless patrons . . . don't just want to be recipients. So the Culinary Cornerstones' six-month training program prepares men and women to succeed in the culinary industry. Participants in the program apply what they learn by beginning to cook, serve, and help run the restaurant.[24]

Do you see what is happening there? As well as immediate needs being attended to, those in need are being encouraged with a 'hand up' in practical ways that enhance their dignity.

I am sure there is great scope to explore how ministries such as food banks can develop towards that same goal.

Doing justice and preaching grace

In this final section of the chapter I want to address the following interrelated questions. What is the relationship between doing economic justice and the church's central calling to proclaim *in words* the good news of Jesus Christ, which people so desperately need to hear? Can these really go hand in hand? What does it mean in practice to 'do justice and preach grace'? It is very important to be clear about these issues, so that we are purposeful in all we do and say, and avoid various potential sources of confusion.

In recent decades many Christians and churches across the world have come to recognize more strongly that Jesus Christ calls his followers *both* to communicate his gospel to those who do not yet know and acknowledge him, *and* to do good. The biblical teaching on the importance of 'word and deed' seems very strong; for example, with regard to the importance of words, after his resurrection Jesus Christ gave a clear statement to his apostles and followers:

> He told them, 'This is what is written: the Messiah will suffer and rise from the dead on the third day, and repentance for the forgiveness of sins will be preached in his name to all nations, beginning at Jerusalem. You are witnesses of these things.'
> (Luke 24:46–48)

This calling and command to *preach* the gospel of repentance and forgiveness of sins is central for God's people in the present age. As the apostle Paul wrote to the disciples in Rome, starting with a quotation from Joel 2:32:

> 'Everyone who calls on the name of the Lord will be saved.'
> How, then, can they call on the one they have not believed in? And how can they believe in the one of whom they have not heard? And how can they hear without someone preaching to them?
> (Rom. 10:13–14)

With regard to the importance of deeds, Jesus Christ also made it crystal clear that his followers were to *obey* all that he had taught them; for example, 'If you love me, you will obey what I command' (John 14:15 NIV 1984).

Christ's Great Commission to the eleven disciples (Matt. 28:18–20) clearly calls his church to 'make disciples', which will require communication by word about his good news; and it also calls all who follow him to 'obey everything I have commanded you'. I do not think I need to say any more.

The more pressing questions are about what it means *in practice* both to communicate (proclaim/preach) the gospel and to do good – especially, in the context of this book, to do justice. Do we do both at the same time? If so, how? Do *some* people in the church do one, and *other* people in the church do the other? But if that is the case, how can they be held together?

At least two ways help us be clear about how *word* and *deed* hold together. One is to be aware that both of these ministries/activities typically involve Christians and churches *in relationships*: often the most fruitful way to be able to share the gospel with people is *as we get to know them*; and to do good to people – especially in supporting those who are poor and needy – involves us in *relationship* with those people.[25] So as we build these relationships with people we should be very clear that we want *both* to do good and support people in their material needs, *and* to take every opportunity to share with them the good news of Christ and his kingdom – which is in reality their deepest need.

The second way is to use the language of *mission* in embracing word and deed, holding them both together under the umbrella, as it were, of mission. Many Christians across the world have accepted this language in recent decades; in particular, many refer to 'integral mission' or 'holistic mission'. This approach argues that Jesus Christ himself uses the language of *mission* (sending), and this includes the mission to which he invites the church – ultimately the mission of *God*.[26] This is perhaps clearest in Christ's prayer to his Father, recorded in John 17. In verses 17–18 he prays for his followers as follows: 'Sanctify them by the truth; your word is truth. As you sent me into the world, I have sent them into the world.'

Jesus Christ, in the world to which his Father sent him, both preached the gospel and ministered to people's material needs; and so, the argument runs, he sends his followers also to do both of these things. This is the mission to which we are called.

Now I am aware that some Christians are not convinced about the merits of using the term 'mission' to include both word and deed: they argue that it is more biblically faithful to limit 'mission' to gospel proclamation (evangelism).[27] I can see some merits in this. In this book, however, I am not seeking to enter that debate. What I will say is that I am persuaded that 'integral mission' and 'holistic mission' are terms that are faithful to the overall thrust of the Bible. But if we take that approach, it is essential that we ensure that word-and-deed ministries really are integrated.

In relation to support for and ministry with people who are poor and needy, I know of at least two churches in London that hold together gospel proclamation and doing good very easily: not only do they offer food on a regular basis to people in need, but they also make it plain to these people that, as part of what happens at that time in the week, they will share with those people something of the good news of Jesus Christ.

If we *fail* to hold these two together, there is the danger that we somehow end up thinking that gospel communication will be done 'by someone else' (but who?) and 'at some other time' (but when?), with the outcome that *no one* ever communicates the gospel to those who need to hear it.[28]

Sharing the gospel may not be the *first* thing we aim to do in relationship with people who are poor and needy, but it is the most crucial thing; and therefore in our planning for work with the poor and needy we must *anticipate*, from the start, ways in which we will be able to communicate the good news of Jesus Christ, in effective ways, with these people.

Then, truly, we will be doing justice and preaching grace.

Conclusion

Local church communities can be beacons of economic justice for the glory of God! This is a biblical vision to inspire us into action. Doing economic justice includes having a special eye open for those who are poor and needy; and in this chapter we have looked at some key biblical principles for how we can support those in material need – both within the church community, and in the wider community. All of this flows out of the gospel – the good news of Jesus Christ and of God's amazing grace. Preaching this gospel and doing economic justice belong together.

Part 1 of this book has focused on how followers of Jesus Christ can do economic justice in our own relationships – as consumers, in the workplace, and in local church communities. In part 2 we will consider how we can do economic justice in our wider society – continuing to move out in a series of concentric circles. The emphasis in the second part will be on the influence that followers of Christ can have *in and through* the organizations and structures of which they are part.

Part 2

DOING ECONOMIC JUSTICE IN AND THROUGH . . .

5
Firms and corporations

The prophet Micah said:

> He [the LORD] has showed you, O man, what is good;
>   and what does the LORD require of you
> but to do justice, and to love kindness,
>   and to walk humbly with your God?
> (Mic. 6:8 RSV)

Introduction

How can we do economic justice in our wider society? In this and the two following chapters the emphasis is on the influence that followers of Christ can have *in and through* the organizations of which they are part. We have great potential to be salt and light (Matt. 5:12–16) in our societies: there are many opportunities for us to do economic justice, and for us to play our part in shaping these institutions and structures so that more economic justice is done. As God moulds us more and more into the likeness of Christ, by his word and Spirit, and as we are thus empowered to do justice and shine for Christ, we can trust that other people will want to find out more about our motivation and passion for all of this. So as we shine for Christ, we will be able to point people to him and his saving grace.

In this chapter we look at doing economic justice in and through firms, companies and corporations. Chapter 3 focused on our own behaviour and relationships in the workplace context. But here in chapter 5 we are focusing on how disciples of Christ can influence the organizations in which they work, and help to lead or manage.

Now at this point some readers may object, 'But I thought that business is all about making profit! How can I possibly get the firm I work for to act more justly? Won't that mean *less* profit?' Those are good questions. But I hope that as we build on the *biblical* understanding of economic justice developed in the first part of the book, we will see that making profit and doing justice can easily go hand in hand. There are plenty of non-Christians in the world of business who believe that having good moral values and making a profit are compatible with each other. How much more should that be so if we believe in the justice-loving God and his good economy!

The core of a biblical understanding of economic justice – as we have seen earlier – is treating people appropriately, according to the norms and principles given by God. This always includes a concern for how the poor and needy are treated. Justice in economic life is *relational*: it is about the quality of relationships between people and between human institutions. And economic justice means that everyone participates in God's blessings, including material blessings. So let us consider how biblical economic justice is to be worked out in the arena of business.[1]

Business: an arena for doing economic justice – or the opposite

Can we build an economy of *both* prosperity *and* justice? The answer is an emphatic 'Yes!' according to the final report of the Commission on Economic Justice [CEJ] (published in 2018).[2] I find this answer very encouraging. But if such an economy is to be built, then it must involve, among other things, what happens in the life of businesses and corporations – for example, in the way that wages and salaries are set, and in the way that firms operate. In other words, business has a key part to play in doing economic justice. As the CEJ put it:

It is not sufficient to seek to redress injustices and inequalities simply by redistribution through the tax and benefit system.

They need to be tackled at source, in the structures of the economy in which they arise. These include the labour market and wage bargaining, the ownership of capital and wealth, the governance of firms, the operation of the financial system and the rules that govern markets. Economic justice cannot be an afterthought; it must be built in to the economy.[3]

If, however, this is to happen, then a crucial role belongs to the people who work in firms and corporations – and especially to the people who help to manage these organizations. Company leaders obviously have great influence 'at ground level' on labour markets and wage bargaining, and on how firms make decisions.

Sometimes when I read publications that call for 'economic justice' – however they define it – I get the impression that the authors think this can come about *only* by the actions of governments and other political institutions: economic justice is seen as something to be built in by political and legal processes. But this approach neglects the biblical emphasis on *relationships*: economic justice is relational – it is about how people are treated, both by other people and by human institutions. Economic justice is not simply a *situation* or *state*; it is also about *doing*, and it is about how we treat one another in relationships.

The same is true for the opposite – that is, for economic *injustice*. When people are mistreated in the economic dimensions of life, then this is *injustice*. And so business is also an arena in which injustice can happen. It is all too easy to think here of examples such as slavery – not only the slavery of earlier centuries, which campaigners such as Wilberforce worked so hard to outlaw, but also modern-day slavery. Oppression of the economically weak – for example, in the form of appalling working conditions, non-payment of wages – can happen at any time.

It follows that business activity is never 'morally neutral'. This is because actions by firms and corporations always involve human relationships; and because this is God's world, in which he – as creator, sustainer and judge – sets all human relationships and behaviour under his perfect moral rule. People are either walking in line with God's moral norms, or they are going against them: there is no 'neutral ground'.

So business is an arena where followers of Jesus Christ can play their part in doing economic justice; and in helping firms and corporations to do economic justice. As members of the body of Christ we can all play a part here – whether directly, if we work for a firm or company, or, if we do not work in such a context, indirectly, by sharing with and praying for those who are involved.

One step: understand your context

What might this look like in practice? Well, it depends to some extent, of course, on what role someone has within a firm or corporation. But let us suppose that you have some kind of senior management or leadership role within a company. The first thing to do is to develop an understanding of the context in your company. Try to gather information about the different dimensions of the firm's activities; especially regarding its various stakeholders – shareholders, employees, customers, suppliers, local communities and the physical environment(s) in which it is located. What can you learn about how the company is behaving towards these different stakeholders?

Then you can begin to think about the kinds of norms and principles given by God for these different relationships. Earlier chapters in this book have offered quite a lot of biblical material here, and you should dig regularly into your Bible in order to keep discovering more. In the light of those norms and principles, how do you think your company is doing? Are there any potential areas where the company may be *mis*treating some of its stakeholders or partners? How much awareness does the firm exhibit of its moral responsibilities in these various dimensions? Overall, how does your company seem to be doing with regard to God's norms for economic justice?

Later in this chapter we will come back to these kinds of questions, and we will consider ways of proceeding from there towards taking actions that would help in doing economic justice. But before that, there is another topic that forms a crucial part of the wider context, and therefore requires our attention: to do with *legal* and *structural* factors at the foundational level of businesses.

The goal(s) of firms and corporations: profits, values and corporate social responsibility

When you hear or read the word 'profits', what thoughts come to mind? For some people, 'profit' is a 'dirty word': it smacks of greed, selfishness, ruthlessness and other wholly negative connotations. For other people, by contrast, to make profits – and even to seek to *maximize* profits – is entirely healthy and virtuous. Professor Milton Friedman (who won the Nobel Prize in Economics; he died in 2006) once wrote, 'In [a free economy] there is one and only one social responsibility of business – to use its resources and engage in activities designed to increase its profits *so long as it stays within the rules of the game.*'[4]

Other people hold opinions at different points along the spectrum between those two positions. There is indeed a vast literature on the relationship between profits, values, the goal(s) of companies and corporate social responsibility. I am not at all seeking to provide an overview of those debates, or to argue for any position. What I do want to show is that to do economic justice can be entirely compatible with making a profit.

One thing to clarify straightaway is the nature of 'profit' (or 'profits'). According to mainstream economic analysis, profit is the excess of revenue (or income) over costs. So in any given year, if a company has total revenue (income) of £100,000, and total costs (before tax) of £80,000, then its profit for that year is £20,000.

If the goal of the company is to maximize its profits, then it will, in Friedman's words, 'use its resources and engage in activities' in such a way as to try to make its profits as large as possible. Typically, this will mean increasing its revenue and/or decreasing its costs. Not surprisingly, life introduces many complexities. One of these is that, in practice, to maximize profits *in the short term* (say, one or two years) may involve the firm in one set of decisions; but to maximize profits *in the long term* (say, five to ten years) may point to a quite different set of strategies! In particular, longer-term strategies are likely to involve deploying funds for *investment*, but the investment may generate a return only after five or ten years. So in the short term the firm may be better off by *not* investing.

What has this to do with economic justice? Well, a desire to *maximize* profits over the next year *could*, logically, suggest a cut in wages, since lower costs mean higher profits, other things being equal,[5] and this could conceivably be regarded as highly *unjust*; especially if the wage cut were focused on the most vulnerable employees (who might be least likely to stand up against the firm). So maximization of profits may be compatible with actions that we could well regard as unjust.

There are, however, other strategies a company can pursue, still consistent with making profits – and perhaps maximizing profits – that would *not* involve it in treating employees, or anyone else, unjustly. For example, this same firm might explore a strategy of investing in employee training, so as to boost the skills and efficiency of its workforce, increase the quality of the goods and services it provides, and hence earn more revenue – whether through increasing the volume it sells, or the price, or both. In this case there is no contradiction between profits and justice – quite the opposite, arguably.

These very simple illustrations are given in order to show that there is no automatic connection between the profits a company makes and the moral (or immoral) nature of the firm's behaviour. Or, to put it more positively, making a profit and doing economic justice can easily go hand in hand.

The legal duty of firms' directors to shareholders[6]

As we continue to explore the relationship between making profits and doing justice, it is important to have some understanding of the real-world context. So we need to take a slight detour and consider briefly some key features of the way that companies and legal frameworks operate. Over recent decades companies and corporations in the Anglo-Saxon world, especially the UK and USA, have given growing emphasis to the responsibilities of companies not only to *shareholders* but also to *stakeholders* as a whole. Shareholders comprise individuals and institutions (e.g. pension funds and insurance companies) who hold financial shares in that company. The term *stakeholders* includes not only shareholders but also employees, customers, suppliers, the local community and the environment.[7] How are these responsibilities to these various parties to be balanced? What happens when there are conflicts between the interests of these different stakeholders – for example, when a firm decides to close a loss-making factory in a location, with consequent impacts upon employees and the local community?[8]

In earlier decades the legal position in the UK and in some other countries was that the primary legal duty of a company was to its owners; that is, the shareholders. (Company law in the UK has for a long time regarded a company as being a legal entity – 'person' – in its own right; that is, distinct from those individuals who work for, manage or hold shares in it.) In economic and financial analysis it was recognized that this legal context meant that, for some companies at least, their goal was *to maximize shareholder wealth*; that is, to run the firm with the objective that its share price was as high as possible. This is sometimes termed 'Shareholder Value Maximization' (SVM). Broadly speaking, SVM and maximization of profits could be seen as very similar and related goals, with maximization of profits being the best way to ensure SVM.[9]

In more recent decades, however, as I mentioned above, increasing attention has been given, both by academics and in decision-making, to the wider group of stakeholders. One of the signs of this has been the growing emphasis on *corporate social responsibility* (CSR). In the UK, CSR is understood as the responsibility of an organization for the impacts of its decisions on society and the environment beyond its legal obligations, through transparent and ethical behaviour.[10] Virtually all the biggest UK companies in the FTSE 100 index now include in their annual reports a section on CSR.[11]

Yet it remains the case that companies that put in a poor performance with regard to *profits* are often very vulnerable to takeover and/or closure. This is so regardless of any virtue or otherwise regarding the firm's CSR performance. Clearly, shareholders still have great influence. This is a key point, whatever the formal legal context. We will come back, later in the chapter, to this vital practical point, since it is crucial with regard to the scope for doing economic justice.

The legal position in the UK, since the passing into law of the Companies Act 2006, is based upon what is termed 'Enlightened Shareholder Value' (ESV), a variant on the SVM discussed above. John Davies puts it as follows:

> In summary these provisions say that directors are (still) expected to manage their companies' affairs in the interests, ultimately, of their members collectively and not of any external parties. Nonetheless, in keeping with the 'enlightened' element of the ESV concept, the law now provides expressly that directors' understanding of what are the best interests of their company is expected to be influenced by their systematic consideration by them of a range of specified 'environmental' factors . . .[12]

So the formal legal position in the UK (at the time of writing, at least) is that what are 'the best interests of a company' is expected to be itself *influenced by* consideration of *those wider factors*. This is a significant way of viewing things.

In practice, the way the wider 'environmental' factors are to be taken into account is as follows. In the course of making their decisions as to how best to promote the success of the company for the benefit of its members as a whole, directors are now required to 'have regard' to each of these matters:

- the likely consequences of any decision in the long term
- the interests of the company's employees
- the need to foster the company's business relationships with suppliers, customers and others
- the impact of the company's operations on the community and the environment

- the desirability of the company maintaining a reputation for high standards of business conduct, and
- the need to act fairly as between members of the company.[13]

In this framework the intention seems clearly to try to push companies towards decisions that reflect a balanced appraisal of all these factors: but still with the overriding consideration being what is in the best interests of the company for the shareholders as a whole. For example, then, if a company, *by failing* to maintain its reputation for high standards of business conduct – the penultimate point in the above list – experiences a reduction in profits, then the directors could be in transgression of the legislation. That is what ESV is about.

In the light of that detour into the complex land of company law, we come back now to the central issue: can companies combine doing economic justice and making profits? Is it possible to do both, *at least in principle*? And once again the answer is a clear 'Yes'. The legal and socio-economic context makes that plain.[14] Profit and other objectives can be considered together by companies.

Now, as noted a little earlier, one of the challenges *in practice* for companies wanting to behave justly is that some shareholders might use their influence to force a company to move away from doing justice, *if* they perceived that the profits performance of that company were, due to the emphasis on just behaviour, being impaired. As I said, we will come back to this vital issue. But for now, let us explore more of what it could look like in reality for firms to do economic justice; and at how disciples of Christ who are in positions of management and leadership might use their influence to encourage this.

Some key areas where companies can do economic justice

There are at least three such areas; no doubt there are more. And, as mentioned earlier, I am not trying to give a detailed 'how to' manual – that is well beyond the scope of this book, and well beyond my capabilities. Instead, I am offering a framework, a way of thinking about doing economic justice, with a view to action.

1 Relationships with employees and workers

Let me start, under this heading, with something that is often not appreciated: simply by helping to provide paid work, firms can help do economic justice! It is a thoroughly biblical principle that people should have work, and that through their paid work people should provide for themselves and their household. This is one of the ways in which people are enabled to participate in God's blessings – especially his material blessings; and that is the fourth element of a biblical understanding of economic justice (see chapter 1). All of this is part of God's created order, and part of his good and just economy.

Therefore, it is important to appreciate the remarkable way in which firms and corporations are able to play this role of helping to provide work and thus contribute to economic justice. I say 'remarkable', because it may not necessarily be the *intention* of an entrepreneur or company director to be playing a part in this way of doing economic justice. Back in the eighteenth century the Scottish philosopher and political economist Adam Smith argued that *markets* in economic life tend to work for the good of all – *but* that the *intention* of people in business is more about their own 'self-interest'. We see that this insight applies also to 'markets' for labour.

Here are some famous words from Adam Smith about this feature of markets:

> It is not from the benevolence of the butcher, the brewer, or the baker, that we expect our dinner, but from their regard to their own interest. We address ourselves, not to their humanity but to their self-love, and never talk to them of our necessities but of their advantages.[15]

Much has been written about this argument put forward by Adam Smith, and about his other related ideas. But the key point here centres on the argument that when someone in business provides a service or product, the rest of us should not delude ourselves into thinking that this is out of sheer generosity. Instead, it is principally out of *self-love* that they keep going in their business. At the end of the day bakers need to be sure that they have earned sufficient revenues to cover their costs and make some profit (i.e. to earn a living, as well as to reinvest in the business, potentially); it is on this that they are likely to be focusing. And yet it is precisely *this* focus ('self-love') that enables you and me to be able to have bread on our table![16]

We should not be unhappy with this emphasis on self-love in this context, I would argue, for a number of reasons. First, there is a proper love for oneself, as well as the love for God and neighbour that God commands of us. Indeed, the second great commandment – as Jesus Christ said – is, 'Love your neighbour as yourself' (Matt. 22:39).[17] (*Not*, we must note, *instead of* yourself.)

Second, there is a proper – and biblical – norm by which people and their households are to provide for themselves. For sure, the New Testament calls disciples of Christ to give generously to others, but it also calls us to earn a living in order to provide for ourselves (see e.g. Eph. 4:28; 1 Tim. 5:8). We can thus appreciate that this is what Adam Smith's baker and butcher are doing.

Third, the sinfulness of human beings must also be kept in mind. The fall is a crucial aspect of a biblical world view. In the light of that it would be foolish to expect that human beings could typically forget any kind of self-love when it comes to economic dealings. More positively, however, there is a case for saying that markets are part of God's wisdom and providence, *especially* for a fallen world; even though self-love may be stronger, since the fall, we can see that, in the context of markets, people can still trade and provide employment in exchange for pay – even if self-love rather than regard for the other is the dominant motivation.

This third point does depend crucially, however, on the different participants in economic dealings having reasonably equal *power*, or at least on participants not *exploiting* any power advantage they may have. In the context of *employment* this point relies, then, on employees and workers having the freedom to move between jobs, rather than being subject only to one employer. The underlying reasoning here is precisely the same as applies to you and me in our choice of which loaf of bread to buy, or, equivalently, as applies to bakers having a range of places in which they could potentially *sell* their produce.

To sum up so far: by helping to provide paid work, firms can help do economic justice. Paid work is a God-given means of people being able to provide for themselves and their household, and thus to participate in God's blessings, and that is biblically one aspect of economic justice. This achievement on the part of firms may not be the first and most direct intention of those who set up a firm or who oversee it, but in God's good providence we can see and appreciate this reality. In addition, many companies *are* aware, whether with greater or lesser clarity, that this is part of their contribution to the wider good.

But there is much more to say about what it means for firms and corporations to do justice in relation to their employees. Indeed, the phrase 'in relation to' is central in a biblical understanding of economic justice, as I have been showing throughout this book. So relationships between an organization and its employees and workers are a vital aspect of economic justice. Any follower of Jesus Christ who has a leadership or management role has the opportunity – and obligation – to influence his or her organization to take this relational dimension seriously.

In chapter 3 we looked at some of the biblical teaching for what it means for an employer to behave towards employees with relational justice. The *relationships* between employers and employees are a vital aspect of doing economic justice, and the quality of these relationships is something on which the Scriptures place great emphasis. There is no need to repeat that material in detail here: some of the key elements and implications concern conditions of work, wages and salaries, and helping employees to develop. If you are in a position of influence in a company, then you must pay careful attention to each of these three aspects, as they are central for doing economic justice.

Since chapter 3 has already explored the implications regarding conditions of work and helping employees to develop, there is no need to say anything further about those aspects in this chapter. Regarding wages and salaries, however, there is more that needs to be considered here, especially by those who are in positions of leadership, and hence influence, within companies. So this takes us to our second main topic area in considering the role of firms and companies in doing economic justice.

2 Wages and salaries

This aspect of doing economic justice is potentially controversial, which is one reason for devoting more time to it now. How is a company to work out what 'justice and fairness' mean with regard to the wages and salaries it pays? Am I suggesting that for each job there is a 'just wage' that can be defined? What about the place of 'flexibility' with regard to the labour market: are 'zero-hours' contracts and other similar arrangements compatible with economic justice? And with regard to some of the deeper and more structural challenges facing an economy such as that of the UK – as highlighted, for example, by the CEJ publications noted at the start of this chapter – how do biblical principles of economic justice apply to those challenges?

The first two of those questions belong together. I am certainly *not* suggesting that for each job there is a 'just wage'. If we want to consider seriously what the biblical material says about economic justice, then we should also accept that – at least on my understanding – what that material gives us is principles and norms: it is then up to us how to apply those principles and norms in practice. (We are to seek God's enabling and wisdom in this as in all other tasks; but we can never presume to declare, 'I know precisely what God wants.') On that basis alone we – as fallen human beings – can never say of any action (call that action 'X'), 'X is *the* just thing to do.' That would be to claim far too much for our own knowledge. So, simply on that reasoning, it would always be unwise to claim that 'for this job £XX is the just wage'. But what we should do is to work hard at letting our minds be guided according to biblical principles and norms for justice.

If we do that, then two dimensions of a biblical understanding of economic justice are especially relevant to the topic of wages and salaries. One is that we must always have a special concern for the poor and needy. The other is that economic justice means that everyone is included in God's blessings, including material blessings. So, especially for people and human organizations, including corporations, which have greater power, these two dimensions should lead those in power to be watchful regarding how they treat those in economically weaker positions, including employees and workers. This is because the default behaviour on the part of fallen human beings, if they have power, is to misuse that power and to exploit those who are weaker. The Bible gives many examples of this – as we have seen earlier in this book.

An economy such as the UK (since 1998), however, has minimum-wage legislation. But how about those in positions of power considering whether or not they should pay something more than that minimum? As we saw in chapter 3, if people (employees) were viewed as an *asset* rather than simply a 'cost', then it would make sense to invest in building up the skills of such people – and this might well mean greater productivity, and hence a higher wage would be appropriate. But also, if the company were in a position to do so, then it might be more in line with principles of justice to increase the pay of the economically weak. We will return to this shortly.

But I can well imagine that, for some readers at least, the following kind of question has come to mind: 'What if my company cannot afford to pay more?' This is clearly a very important consideration. In a competitive *product* market – that is, the market into which the firm seeks to sell the goods and services it produces – the 'profit margin' is often very small. (The profit margin is the excess of revenue over costs.) One element of this very small ('thin') profit margin is that all competitors have to work hard at keeping their costs down – and that includes labour costs. If the costs incurred by any given firm (call it firm 'A') go up – relative to their competitors – then firm A will not be able to survive. If it raises the selling price, then the close competition means that many consumers will probably switch to buying the output of *other* firms. And in that case firm A will see its sales and revenue decrease; and it may well then end up making losses. That would not be sustainable.

This is a significant consideration. In these sorts of circumstances it is valid to place some reliance on what people often term 'the going wage' or the 'market wage' (i.e. the wage rate that is normal for a job), even at low levels of pay. With regard to the *wages* aspect of how to treat employees who are economically weak, it may well be that, for a firm in these sorts of circumstances, to act justly (Col. 4:1) means paying more or less the going wage rate. But the firm should also be ensuring that in the general working conditions, and in viewing people as assets, they are treating employees well.

A good number of companies, however, do *not* face such fierce competition in the product market.[18] For these, there may well be scope to explore whether or not a higher wage might be paid to those who are economically weak. Recall that the biblical basis for this would be, in part, having a concern for the poor and needy; and there is the key point that, in a fallen world, we should – sadly – always have an awareness that those with power are likely to be exploiting those who have little power. And therefore this awareness reinforces the practical importance of having a special eye out for those who are in the weakest economic position. In other words, do *not* assume that your company is likely to be doing the right thing! And, more positively, *do* use your influence to try to make your organization more attentive to the moral importance of treating justly those who are weakest.

3 Labour market flexibility

Another aspect of wages and salaries concerns the place of 'flexibility' with regard to the labour market: are 'zero-hours' contracts and other similar arrangements compatible or incompatible with economic justice? This has become quite a contentious area in recent years, not least in the UK, and much has been written about it.[19] There is insufficient space to go into detail here. But there are two key factors to bear in mind. First, flexibility in the labour market – the ability of firms and workers to have a greater range of working arrangements, and for people to move between jobs more speedily – can help to bring a number of benefits in the efficiency of an economy, and hence in how much it can produce.

Here is a simple example. In events management some of the work comes at specific times – for example, setting up a stage in the afternoon before an evening concert, and then taking it down late at night. This is far from a regular nine-to-five job. So *if* there are workers who are willing to be paid for a few hours, at a rate of pay to which they agree without any force, then this is cheaper for the events management company than having to employ people in permanent nine-to-five jobs. The outcome is that concert prices should be cheaper than would otherwise be the case; and therefore there will probably be more concerts, and more attenders, than would otherwise be the case.

The second factor, however, is that the quality of relationships is still central, according to biblical economic justice. The danger with increased 'flexibility' is that it can give more scope for powerful companies to exploit people (workers) who are in a weak bargaining position. It is thus crucial to assess the details of how these two factors play out together in any given context: to some extent they are in tension with one another. In my view it is not reasonable to conclude with a general 'Yes, it is fine' or a general 'No, it is bad' regarding labour market flexibility, including zero-hours contracts. Certainly, it is crucial that the workers involved must agree to the arrangements: if there is oppressive conduct on the part of the employer, then that is clearly unjust.

In the light of the tension between these two factors it is important to keep under review what is happening on the ground regarding labour market flexibility.

4 Shareholder power in conflict with justice?

At this point there is an additional practical concern, and I have hinted at this a couple of times already in this chapter. It may be that a company has some scope to pay a somewhat higher wage to those who are in the weakest position, but what if the *shareholders* and/or potential shareholders use *their* economic power to undermine a corporation that adopted such a policy? In other words, if the company is quoted on the stock market – as opposed to being owned privately – then it could be vulnerable to large reductions in its share price, through shareholders selling shares in large quantities.[20] In this case the company could eventually be taken over by a different set of people/institutions – who would presumably *not* favour the policy of paying higher wages to employees in a weak position.

This 'market for corporate control' is a key factor in an economy such as that of the UK, where a significant proportion of companies have their shares traded on stock markets. And the same vulnerability to takeover could, if a firm has a drop in actual or expected profits, come into play *whatever* the perceived cause of its worsened profits performance – whether higher wages (as above), or by the firm giving greater attention to the interests of *other* external stakeholders, or by poor management, or other factors.

What is a corporation to do if it considers that were it to take a more just approach to employees in a weak position, it would be vulnerable to takeover?

This is not some far-fetched concern. The market for corporate control is a reality that directors and senior managers of companies have to take into account all the time. And the case I have been considering – whether or not to pay higher ('above market rate') wages to the economically weakest employees – could in practice easily make a firm vulnerable. It is, in other words, another way in which companies may perceive that to do justice is something they cannot afford. What should a company do in this type of situation?

I would *not* suggest that directors and senior managers ignore this concern. It is surely wise to try to build a company that exhibits just moral behaviour *in a way that is sustainable*. So practicalities must be fully taken into account. Here are a few things for the leadership to bear in mind. First, they can talk with major shareholders about the direction in which they would like to take the company. They can remind shareholders of the obligations, recognized in law (see above), that a company has to its various stakeholders. Second, they can seek, as far as possible, to ensure that paying higher wages to economically weak employees will *enhance* the performance of the firm, in due course. Third, they can inform the wider public, including current and potential consumers, about their desire to exhibit just values – this could quite easily result in some people choosing to purchase *more* of this company's output than would otherwise be the case. (This is the opposite effect from that of a 'consumer boycott'.)

Fourth, there are some longer-term structural options that a company could consider. In his book *Firm Commitment* Professor Colin Mayer puts forward an option he labels the 'trust firm':

> A trust firm is a corporation that has a board of trustees who are the guardians of the corporation's stated values and principles . . . [T]hey do not interfere in the day-to-day running of the firm, but do ensure that the firm has clearly articulated values and principles *and abides by them*.[21]

As Professor Mayer explains, the John Lewis Partnership in the UK is one case of this type of company structure.

This structure cannot be created overnight, and it will not suit all markets or industries. But it is a very creative and attractive proposal, already practised in some corporations.

The third and final topic area to consider, regarding the role of firms and corporations in doing economic justice, has become contentious in recent years: it is about the pay (including salaries and bonuses) given to the top corporate executives.

5 Corporate executive pay

At the opposite end of the earnings scale from the most economically weak employees are the senior executives. Especially in the years following the financial and economic crisis which began in 2007, there has been increasing concern, in many quarters, about what often seem to be extremely lucrative salary/bonus schemes awarded to senior executives. Why is this a relevant concern in the context of biblical economic justice? It is because of the biblical emphasis on *everyone* participating in God's blessings, including material blessings. So, to be clear, the concern here is *not* about envy. Envy – a longing to possess something awarded to or achieved by another – is not at all the same as a concern for justice. And envy is condemned in the Bible (e.g. Prov. 14:30; Mark 7:22; Rom. 1:29). The question regarding corporate executive pay, with justice in mind, is to what extent the payments made are compatible with everyone participating in God's blessings.

A number of factors should be kept in mind in seeking an answer to that question. The first is that it is important to gain some understanding of what is happening, and why, regarding corporate executive pay. It is easy to rush in and condemn, especially when the amounts paid are sometimes extremely large. So what is happening? In 2017 the average pay for a UK CEO (chief executive officer) was £4.5 million.[22] In 2014 in the UK the average pay ratio between FTSE 100 CEOs and the average wage of their employees was 148:1. This compared to a ratio of 47:1 in 1998.[23] A similar trend occurred in the USA. These trends seemed to take off during the 1980s, and then continued. In the USA over the period 1978 to 2014 CEO pay was almost 1,000 times higher in 2014 than in 1978; during that same time period typical worker pay rose by only 10.9%.[24] These are astonishing differences.

But *why* is this happening? This is much harder to fathom.[25] A number of explanations have been put forward – but this book is not the place to review all of these. Between 1980 and 2011 the average value of American firms rose by 425%; during the same period the average rise in CEO pay in America's largest firms was 405%. So it seems that, in one way or another, the rise in CEO pay is connected with the growth in stock market values of large corporations.[26]

This suggests that the large increases in corporate executive pay are a symptom of one of the widely noted features of *globalization*, namely that since the 1970s the benefits of higher income across the world have *not* been shared – instead, a small number of organizations and individuals have experienced huge increases in their income.

The second factor to bear in mind is that there has been increasing concern, including within corporate and financial circles, regarding the large size of the increases in CEO pay, relative to the earnings of other people. This concern resonates to some extent with the emphasis on *everyone* participating in God's material blessings, presented by a biblical understanding of economic justice. For example, an article in the *Financial Times* in February 2017, reviewing trends over the previous twenty-five years, included the following candid comment: 'Executive greed has been indulged by boards nervous of losing top talent and [by] an industry of remuneration consultants that has thrived on an arms race to design top-quartile pay packages.'[27] Such open and unqualified talk of 'greed' among corporate executives, in the columns of the *Financial Times*, is striking. In chapter 6 I will return to the issue of greed, especially in the context of banks and other financial institutions – but for now we should note that the question of greed has become relevant across the whole corporate sector, not only in the financial dimension.

Other analysts have suggested that some of the incentive packages developed since the early 1990s have encouraged decisions based primarily on *short-term* considerations – for the company as well as corporate executives – to the detriment of the longer-term good of the company.[28]

These concerns resonate with the biblical emphasis on everyone sharing in God's blessings, including material blessings. That emphasis raises concerns about two related issues: first, regarding chief executives receiving huge material rewards when many employees in their companies receive only small increases in pay; and, second, regarding the extent to which large corporations have been operating to generate huge increases in shareholder wealth, perhaps without sufficient regard to the interests of a wider group of stakeholders. This latter aspect obviously connects with the discussion earlier in this chapter about the goals of corporations, and the balance between shareholders and other stakeholders.

Those concerns lead us to the third factor to be kept in mind, as we ask to what extent the payments made to corporate executives are compatible with an emphasis on everyone participating in God's blessings. We can present this third factor in the form of a question. What could be done differently? In other words, for people who are in senior leadership and management positions in corporations – especially those who are followers of Christ – how can a biblical understanding of economic justice inform their decisions? Here are a few practical things to consider. If someone is offered a huge salary/bonus package, how does this package fit with a biblical emphasis on everyone participating in God's material blessings? Is the company generating, and is it likely to generate, improvements in the livelihood of *all* employees, for example? If not, to what extent is the salary/bonus package justified?

Something else to consider is this: what scope is there for the salary/bonus package to be renegotiated in a *downwards* direction? If the highly paid corporate executive were to ask for that, what might the reactions and responses be? There might conceivably be some sense in which shareholders might be *unhappy* about such a renegotiation, and if so, that would need to be taken into account.

A further thing to consider is the possibility of the company undertaking a more thorough and strategic review of its own goals and practices: a hiatus around a corporate pay package might be a catalyst for the company to reappraise its commitment to *all* of its employees, over the next planning period. This would be a more positive way of exploring what the firm could do in practice to operate in such a way that everyone involved participated in God's material blessings.

Conclusion

In an interview billionaire Christian and businessman David Green was asked about how he, as a Christian, saw the relationship between doing business, making money and giving money away. The interview piece, published on the *Christian Today* website on 27 April 2017 by Jeremy Bowyer, is entitled, 'Are Christians Allowed to Get Rich? Billionaire Christian Shares His View on Business and Making Money'. Bowyer writes:

> Like so many Christian business leaders I've met over the years, David found at least a partial vindication in philanthropy. Yes,

missionaries might be better than entrepreneurs, but at least entrepreneurs can cut big checks to missionaries. Business becomes spiritually acceptable via the collection plate. I've seen and heard many executives who believe that the portion of profit which you gave to holy callings rendered the rest of the 'secular' business enterprise, if not fully holy, at least acceptable.

It was not until later that Green saw that when we're at business, we can already be 'about my father's business' . . . even before any of the earnings were given away. He was already engaging in the great commission (to disciple the nations) when he treated workers well and taught workers to treat customers well.[29]

To treat workers well is indeed central to being a disciple of Jesus Christ and a child of our heavenly Father, and it is a central part of doing economic justice. David Green's example helps to show the great potential in the hands of Christians in leadership in the world of business – potential to influence their firms and corporations to do justice. And all of this to the glory of God by shining for Jesus Christ.

6

Banks and other financial institutions

Jesus Christ said, 'You cannot serve both God and Money.'[1] The apostle Paul wrote, 'Those who want to get rich fall into temptation and a trap and into many foolish and harmful desires that plunge people into ruin and destruction. For the love of money is a root of all kinds of evil' (1 Tim. 6:9–10a). The prophet Isaiah said:

> Then you shall see and be radiant;
>   your heart shall thrill and exult,
> because the abundance of the sea shall be turned to you,
>   the wealth of the nations shall come to you.
> (Isa. 60:5 esvuk)

Introduction

'Doing economic justice in and through wealthy banks? Are you having a laugh? That's not what banks are for!' That may well be the reaction of many people at this point. Perhaps it is possible for businesses that *produce goods* and *useful services* to do some measure of justice, as we saw in the previous chapter, but can anyone seriously suggest that banks and other financial institutions could be vehicles for economic justice? Surely these financial giants are simply about making money?

Certainly, it is a major challenge for *anyone* to consider how to be a positive influence for economic justice in the arena of banks and financial institutions; and we must not underestimate this challenge. For one thing, there can be little doubt that, for at least a significant number of people who enter the world of finance, a major motivation is to get rich. A quick skim through books about the financial world, and the finance columns of newspapers, makes that plain. In addition, the vast sums of money some people earn in the world of finance seem to make that world a particularly attractive one if getting rich is your aim. And if that is someone's main aim, then it is easy to see how the idea of *doing justice* at the same time could get pushed a long way down the priority list.

But this challenge is even greater for followers of Jesus Christ. The verses from the New Testament, quoted above, present a stark choice and a serious warning: 'You cannot serve both God and Money'; 'Those who want to get rich fall into temptation and a trap . . .' So to work in an arena where for many people the goal *is* to get rich, and where the love of money is very evident, is a decision that followers of Christ must weigh up carefully. I am not, of course, suggesting that this arena is somehow a no-go area for Christians. Christ sends his followers 'into the world' (John 17:16–18). And we would therefore expect Christ to call some of his followers to work in the finance arena. But my point here is that for us to seek to *do justice* in *this* arena is probably to choose one of the most challenging contexts available. Not only will we need much grace and wisdom from God simply to avoid being dragged away from love of God into the love of money, but we will need much grace and wisdom also in seeking to promote economic justice, when for many people around us that is not a major concern.

In this chapter we will look at three different topics in the arena of banking and finance. For each of these, challenges regarding economic justice are very important. First, we will consider *excessive lending, borrowing and debt*: the problems here came to the fore at the time of the financial and economic crisis that began in 2007–8, but has had enormous impacts more than a decade later. How does this topic link to *economic justice*? Because if banks and others lend excessively, they are failing in their *relational responsibility* to borrowers – as, potentially, are the borrowers in theirs; and, as we saw in chapter 1, how people are treated in relationships is a key dimension of biblical economic justice. Second, we look at a closely related topic, which is the way in which banks and other financial institutions *treat those who are economically weak* ('the poor and needy', in biblical language), and here the focus will be on high-interest loans, such as 'payday loans'.

Third, we will consider some more deeper issues to do with underlying attitudes and values. We will look at *greed*, especially in the context of banks and other financial institutions. In biblical terms greed is plainly displeasing to God, as it is a form of wickedness and often goes alongside the doing of *injustice* – it is thus opposite to the righteousness and justice God requires of people. And connected to that, we need to think about how and why *folly* and *pride* seem especially prevalent in banks and other financial institutions – especially those that are huge. Again these are, as we will see, the opposite of the righteousness and justice God demands of us. So we must consider both how pride and folly prevent the doing of justice, and how all of this can be overcome by the life-giving power of the gospel.

In considering all of these topics and challenges, the overall aim of this chapter is to help equip followers of Jesus Christ to be a good influence in and through banks and other financial institutions, working for economic justice. As with the role of Christians in firms and corporations – as considered in the previous chapter – this influence may be more or less direct: some Christians will be employed in banks and other financial institutions, and some in senior positions of responsibility; others will be able to support these people through prayer, advice and encouragement; and there may also be a role to be played by shareholders and through campaigns of various kinds. As we work now for what is just, we do so in the light of the new heaven and earth God will bring about, at the end of this age; and, remarkably, in that new heaven and earth – as foreseen by the prophet Isaiah in the words quoted above (see also Rev. 21:24) – the 'wealth of the nations' will be present.

Excessive lending, borrowing and debt: a failure of relational justice

In chapter 1 we saw that the biblical teaching places reciprocal responsibilities on borrowers and lenders. A biblical understanding of economic justice regarding borrowers and lenders shows that there is a vital package of norms and principles we must apply today. Borrowers have a responsibility to repay. Lenders have a responsibility to treat borrowers with mercy and dignity; and, instead of lifelong servitude due to debt, there is a fundamental principle of release from burdensome debt, and hence a principle of *hope*. In the twenty-first-century world, especially in the West, the socio-economic context is very different from that of the Old Testament. Nevertheless, as earlier chapters have argued, this package of underlying norms and principles given by God still applies in our context.

As we think about the contemporary context, it is crucial to appreciate the relational dimension of lending and borrowing. Even though some modern-day banks are colossal in size – with any one person or household tiny in comparison – those biblical principles continue to hold. We live in a *moral* universe, God's universe. Moreover, by taking this key point on board, we are able to critique the idea – noted in the introduction above – that the large banks and financial institutions simply exist to make a profit, to make money. All firms and corporations, including banks, have moral responsibilities under God, whether or not they acknowledge him. Even if some leaders of financial institutions consider that the *only* thing that matters to them is maximizing profit and wealth, they still have those moral responsibilities, whether or not they recognize them; and God will one day hold all of us to account for the ways in which we have discharged our responsibilities.

So what happens when there is 'excessive' lending and borrowing? Who has moral responsibility? What do we mean by 'excessive' lending and borrowing? Who is to say how much is excessive? How can anyone know, ahead of time, how much is excessive? And finally, when the debt burden has become too large – so that people are unable to repay – what should be done? These are the crucial and interrelated questions we must consider.

The famous economist John Maynard Keynes once wrote, 'If you owe your bank a hundred pounds, you have a problem. But if you owe your bank a million pounds, it has.' In more recent times, *The Economist* newspaper offered the following additional insight: 'If you owe your bank a billion pounds everybody has a problem.'[2]

These problems arise, of course, only when someone owes whatever the amount is, *and is struggling to repay*. This problem may or may not have been foreseen ahead of time. In the case of the financial crisis that began in 2007–8, it is now widely accepted that the financial institutions that engaged on a large scale in so-called 'sub-prime' lending, in the years before the crisis broke, *should* have known better.[3] In any case, banks today do recognize, by and large, that *they* have a responsibility to try to ensure that the potential *borrower* does have the means to repay a loan that is being considered. (The borrower also has responsibility here, as we have already established.) In theory, that ought to mean that banks do not lend excessively. But sometimes they do! So the 'theory' requires further investigation.

As we engage with this issue of excessive lending, borrowing and debt, there are, as I said, a number of interrelated factors and questions we must consider.

How lenders assess risk – and what they do with this information

First, any loan clearly has some element of risk associated with it. If B (the borrower) seeks to borrow from A, with a commitment to repay, then there is automatically a *future* dimension to this relationship: and no mortal human being can *know* the future. If A is a bank, then there are likely to be a large number of such loans for it to assess. Some will have a higher degree of future risk (as assessed *now*); others a lower risk.[4] Quite often the interest rate charged to a given borrower will to some extent reflect the risk (a 'risk premium' is included), and will therefore be higher than for other borrowers or loans. And for some loans, such as a mortgage, the lender has a back-up ('security'): if the borrower fails to repay, then the lender is legally empowered to take the 'secured asset' – for example, the house itself. Such 'secured' loans help to lessen the overall risk for the *lender*.

Bank A will typically operate in line with some maximum overall level of risk: if some potential borrower C involves a risk higher than that maximum, then A will not offer a loan to C. (Risk will include a number of variables, including the income of the potential borrower, his or her location, age, etc.)

Bearing all of the above points in mind, it would clearly be silly to say that *any* degree of risk (above zero) is 'excessive'. But what, then, is 'excessive' risk?

'Excessive' risk

A reasonable way for a lender, such as Bank A, to proceed would be – as we have just seen – to make loans only if the measured risk is below some maximum threshold. (Even if a higher interest rate is charged, as a risk premium, there will still be a maximum threshold of risk that a lender will permit.) This is sensible on the part of the lender, as well as being sensible for the potential borrower. However, as already mentioned, sometimes lenders offer loans that can be seen to be unduly risky. The 'sub-prime' lending ahead of 2007 is a case in point; but there are plenty of other examples of this. So 'excessive' risk effectively means a level of risk at which there is a *substantial* likelihood that a *significant* proportion of borrowers will be unable to repay. Clearly, lenders have to make operational – that is, numerical/statistical – measures of what counts as 'substantial' and 'significant'.

The official authorities (regulators) also keep an eye on this – assuming they take on such a regulatory role. But there is still a *moral* responsibility on the part of the lenders, whatever the role of the regulatory bodies.

In reality, there are times when lenders, taken as an overall group, relax (i.e. increase) the threshold maximum level of risk. Now this may mean that only *some* lenders increase their risk threshold. Is this imprudent on their part? Now we are getting to the heart of the matter. Bank D, for example, may consider that it can *afford* the higher risk; for example, it will have strategies and financial cushions for covering missed payments and 'bad debts'. In that sense, Bank D may consider its actions to be prudent. *But what about the borrowers?* This is the crunch question. And this is where the *relational* understanding of what is happening is so important. If Bank D lends to someone, *knowing* that there is a significant probability that the person will struggle to repay, then Bank D *has failed in its relational responsibility.* This takes us to a third set of factors.

Powerful lenders, weaker borrowers: weighty responsibility

As shown earlier, borrowers have a responsibility to repay. That is plain from the biblical material. This implies a responsibility to take out a loan *only* after careful consideration.[5] (The case of 'emergency loans' – lending to someone who is in desperate need – is in a different category; and we will come to that in the next main section.) So when I suggest that the lender also has a responsibility, this does not detract from the borrower's responsibility. But it does mean that they *both* have a responsibility. Why is this? Greater power typically brings with it greater responsibility, in moral terms. And this is especially so in a lender–borrower relationship, if the lender is more powerful than the borrower.

Large lenders know full well what they are doing when they conduct marketing campaigns to promote 'special loan deals', 'loans to suit your every need', and so on. And, if they are making loans that are approaching, or going above, that risk threshold we discussed just now, then they know full well, again, what they are doing. The large lender can afford some 'bad debts'; but for any given borrower, a 'bad debt' is not a statistic: it is their whole life. Debt problems very often dominate a person and their household: they affect their family relationships, employment, stress levels and health. But precisely because lenders are *in a relationship* with the borrower, and because the lender is powerful in that relationship, the lender has a responsibility that cannot be ducked. If I am in a position of power in relation to someone else, I have to be careful how I exercise that power – it is a moral responsibility.

Therefore, if powerful lenders make loans that have excessive risk, as defined above, then they are *not* treating the potential borrowers appropriately and are misusing their power. And to mistreat someone in this way is incompatible with economic justice. In other words, such lenders are acting unjustly.

When such lenders utilize marketing campaigns to try to persuade people to take up such loan offers, the marketing becomes part of the problem. We are all familiar with such campaigns for all manner of goods and services; and in a sense we as consumers tacitly go along with these campaigns – in watching the adverts, we are allowing the producers to try to influence us. With regard to loans, however, the danger of marketing campaigns is much greater. If the lending is linked with excessive risk, then the people who take up such loans are putting themselves and potentially their whole livelihood at risk, as I mentioned just now. So, deliberately to try to persuade people to take such risk is highly *irresponsible*. Lenders have no excuse here. The marketing of loans with excessive risk only adds to the injustice of the lenders' behaviour.

Expansion in lending: the wider macroeconomic context

In trying to understand what happens when there is excessive lending, another aspect must be taken into account. This has to do with the wider macroeconomic context. So a short piece of economic analysis, which I trust is not too daunting, is needed.

If we think of borrowers and lenders as a market, then it is important to understand the demand and supply aspects. In the case of borrowers and lenders the thing 'supplied' and 'demanded' is *money*; more precisely, it is what one can term 'loanable funds'. That is, loanable funds are what lenders have to offer – money that they are willing to lend. And loanable funds are what borrowers are seeking to obtain. So we need to think about what factors influence the *supply* of loanable funds, and what factors influence the *demand* for loanable funds.

As in any market – so long as the market functions reasonably well – there are incentives on the part of all participants for demand and supply to be more or less equal. After all, borrowers do not want to be told by a bank, 'Sorry, we have run out of funds for mortgages.' And no lender wants to have spare cash lying around, on which they cannot earn much return: they would much rather lend it out at interest. Indeed, since they typically have to *pay* interest to those who deposit funds with them (savers), then if any of these funds are *not* lent out at interest – or otherwise invested for some prospective return – then the lenders make a *loss* with these funds.

One of the things that helps demand and supply to come into line, in *all* markets, is the ability of the *price* to adjust up and down. In the case of the market for apples, for example, if there is a glut of apples, due perhaps to a bumper harvest, then the market price will drop, which is likely to induce people to purchase more apples than they would otherwise have done.

What, then, is the 'price' of loanable funds? It is the interest rate for those funds. In effect, the interest rate is the price, or at least part of the price, someone pays out in exchange for receiving a loan. And it is also the price (return) lenders receive in exchange for providing a loan. Therefore one of the key elements in the market for loanable funds is the rate of interest. If there is a glut of funds available, then – other things being equal – lenders will seek to offer loans at a *lower* interest rate than otherwise, in order to attract higher demand.

How does this relate to the possibility of 'excessive' risk? It is extremely relevant, at least on occasions. Suppose that on the macroeconomic scale there is a large increase in loanable funds. In other words, there is a large increase ('glut') in savings – money that is received but not spent. In such a situation it is likely that at least some of those savings (loanable funds) will be deposited with banks – especially in the West. In that case *banks will be keen to lend out these additional funds.* But to whom will they lend them? If demand was equal to supply before the savings glut, and now there is additional supply, where will the additional demand come from? How can people and/or companies be induced to borrow more?

In these circumstances we would expect the average rate of interest to fall; and that might help to generate demand. But it is important to dig deeper here. We should look at who may borrow additional funds. And one possibility here – especially with a *large* increase in loanable funds – is that some lenders will try to offer loans, at very low short-term interest rates, to *higher-risk* borrowers. (Unless the interest rate [price] were cut, people in this category would not be able to afford additional borrowing.) In other words, financial institutions may choose to lend money to 'sub-prime' borrowers.

This is exactly what happened in the run-up to the financial crisis that began in 2007–8. Here is what I wrote near the time (in a 2010 paper):

Essentially, as the twenty-first century began to unfold, the USA and other Western economies have been spending far more than they have been earning. This is so not only for the governments: the corporate and personal sectors have also been borrowing. So the USA in particular has been running an enormous deficit in its external trade. But from where have the funds come to finance all this? The answer is: from China, in particular, and also others of the 'emerging economies'. China and the other emerging economies have been building up financial reserves – especially reserves held in the form of US dollars – on a very large scale. In other words, they have been *saving*, in enormous quantities.

This 'glut' of savings has led to two major developments in the West: 'sub-prime' lending and financial bubbles (unsustainable increases in the prices of financial assets and of property). These are interrelated. Part of the attraction of sub-prime lending/borrowing was that, in the light of rising house prices, the risks of such lending and borrowing *seemed* to be low: houses could always (it felt) be sold at a profit, and hence mortgage loans could safely be paid off. The argument is, then, that the sub-prime lending and financial bubbles in the West had their origins in the global economic imbalances. The explanation is now widely accepted.[6]

What is the point of all this analysis of background factors in the global economy? The point is that individual lenders can be very strongly affected by the macroeconomic context. Their decisions are not taken in a vacuum: they are under pressure to respond to what is happening in the wider setting. For example, as I said earlier, if banks have surplus funds they do not lend out, then they are likely to make a *loss* with those funds. This is obviously a serious situation for such banks.

So it is important to understand something of the wider context, when we are thinking about what happens regarding loans that carry excessive risk.

Nevertheless, to understand the context is *not* to condone reckless behaviour. Far from it. The clear framework of moral responsibility – on both borrowers and lenders – I set out earlier still applies. And, since large lenders have a greater responsibility – as I argued earlier – then that still applies as well. So regarding the 'sub-prime' lending in the first decade of the twenty-first century (especially in the USA), those who promoted and provided these loans carry a heavy moral responsibility. Excessively risky lending that plunges households into grave debt difficulties is a moral failure on the part of the lenders.

As I said earlier, borrowers also have some responsibility in such a situation. But the greater blame rests on those who promoted and provided the loans. In the framework of economic justice that governs relationships between lenders and borrowers, to lend at excessive risk in these ways is a form of injustice.

Burdensome debt: the principle of release and hope

Finally, we come to the vital question of what is to be done when someone's debt has become burdensome. We have looked at what happens – and why – with excessive lending and borrowing, at some background macro factors, at the responsibilities on both borrowers and lenders, and at the injustice on the part of powerful lenders when they engage in excessive lending. But having considered all of that, we must face the question of what is to be done when debt has become burdensome. And here the biblical material gives us the powerful principle of *release and hope*.

To cancel a debt is costly for the lender. I lend you £50; if you are unable to pay it back, and I cancel the debt, it costs me £50. The lender must absorb the full cost of the unpaid debt. (This makes debt forgiveness a powerful metaphor for the forgiveness of *sin*, as in, for example, the Lord's Prayer recorded in Matthew's Gospel, Matt. 6:11.) The Bible gives us a clear principle of debt cancellation: this is plain in Deuteronomy 15:1–11, as we saw in chapter 1. For the Old Testament Israelites, every seventh year was a year of debt cancellation and release.[7] This would come at a cost to the lender, but for the borrower what joy and release!

Here we have a powerful principle of release and hope. Borrowers would never have to face a lifetime of debt servitude. Instead, they could find sure hope in the guaranteed release that was coming – and coming in seven years or under. And this release was *unconditional*: it was not limited only to certain types of borrowers, or to cases where borrowers had made 'special efforts' to repay. All debts were to be cancelled unconditionally in that seventh year.

In our twenty-first-century context we are not bound by the specifics of the Old Testament laws: but from them – as argued throughout this book – we can derive social and economic principles that *do* apply to us. And so we have this principle of debt release and hope. This balances with the principles of justice and mercy we have also seen in the biblical material regarding the relationship between lenders and borrowers.

Please note that I am *not* saying that in today's world *all* loans must be only for a maximum of seven years – that would wipe out the mortgage market, for example! Nor that, in today's world, *all* debts, of any kind – including domestic property mortgages – should be cancelled every seven years. Such a policy would, similarly, destroy the mortgage market. As I have already said, in our twenty-first-century context we are not bound by the specifics of the Old Testament laws. It is the principles that apply to us. And in the case of the debt cancellation every seventh year, as in Deuteronomy 15, this was given in the context of *compassionate* loans, not commercial loans. So if you have a mortgage of, say, fifteen or twenty-five years, please do *not* think that economic justice means it will be cancelled after only seven years!

We have seen here principles of justice, mercy, release and hope. What will the application of these mean in our day? How does this set of principles impact on lenders and borrowers? We have been looking at the issue of *excessive* lending and borrowing, because this is such a significant feature of what has been happening in the banking sector in recent times. The principle of debt release means that lenders must accept that borrowers should be released from *burdensome* debts – whether these have come about as a consequence of excessive lending and borrowing, or as a consequence of any other factors.

In practice this will mean the lender and the borrower communicating with one another, and ideally sitting together to work out a way forward. To sit together speaks of a *relationship* between lender and borrower. Some readers may respond, 'That can never work when you have banks of an enormous size.' But it can and must work: large institutions still have relationships, both internally and externally, because their most significant component is *people*. So if a borrower is in difficulty with a debt owed to a giant-sized bank, it is entirely feasible for the bank to appoint an individual within its ranks to talk to this borrower.

The way forward for a borrower who is in difficulty must include some potential for debt cancellation, at least for some portion of the debt. The principle here is release and hope: an unmanageable and permanent debt burden is incompatible with that principle.

By shining the spotlight on the issues of excessive lending, borrowing and debt – as we have been doing in this section – the challenges brought by a biblical understanding of justice are seen to be stark. Yet challenges also bring opportunities. And so there is an important opportunity for followers of Jesus Christ to play key roles, directly and indirectly, in influencing the ways that banks and financial institutions deal with these challenges.

We turn now to a second crucial set of challenges in this arena of finance.

Treatment of those who are economically weak: high-interest loans (credit)

This is what a man from the West Midlands who applied to a high-interest credit company for a payday loan said:

> I was surprised when they said yes, given everyone else had turned me down – I was even more surprised when the £250 I borrowed went up to £499 in a flash. And of course, all of a sudden I found myself in even more debt, my problems worsened. They should've turned me down, for my own sake.

This is from a case study, part of a report (*Life on Debt Row*) published in 2018 by the Royal Society for Public Health.[8] Many examples could be given of this kind of experience: of people in tight economic circumstances who are offered a high-cost loan, and then bitterly regret both the initial decision and what happened to them. 'Payday loans' are only one type of high-cost loans (or credit) – they are given the term 'payday' because their duration is typically less than one month; and so your next payday is when you are expected to pay back the loan.

The high-cost credit company that made the loan to the man quoted above is still trading (at the time of writing). One notorious 'payday loan' company in the UK, Wonga, went into administration (ceased trading) at the end of August 2018. But the high-cost credit sector as a whole seems to have plenty of life in it.

As we look into this topic of high-interest loans, one obvious question comes to mind: if loans to the 'sub-prime' borrowers, as discussed above, can be made at *low* interest, why are payday loans and the like offered at such *high* interest rates? It is important to deal with this question at the start. The answer is essentially to do with whether or not the loan is *secured*. In the cases of 'sub-prime' mortgages, the loans were secured on the property (e.g. house) that was mortgaged; so in the case of non-repayment the lender had the legal right to take control of that property and the borrower would lose it. In the case of high-cost credit, however, the loan is *unsecured*; here the risk facing the lender – of non-payment – is covered by the fact of the high interest and other fees charged.

The size of the interest rates and fees that can be charged is mind-bogglingly high. With Wonga at the end of December 2014, more than three years before it ceased trading, its quoted representative annual percentage rate (APR) was no less than *1,509%*! And this was *after* the official regulator – the Financial Conduct Authority [FCA] – had stepped in to place a cap (upper limit) on interest rates, fees and charges in this high-cost credit sector. Before the FCA's intervention Wonga's APR was almost four times higher: 5,853%.[9] Whether before or after the FCA's action, these rates are scarily high.

The FCA had previously said the price caps meant that someone taking out a £100 loan for 30 days and paying it back on time would not pay more than £24 in charges.[10] This sounds innocuous at first. But it is still equivalent to an APR of over 1,500%! And the reality is that to borrow £100 and have to pay back that £100 plus another £24, within 30 days, is an extremely expensive form of credit. Yet many individuals and households in the UK are frequently accessing such high-cost credit. They also tend to be, however, individuals and households on low incomes, and therefore economically weak.[11]

The contrast between God's Old Testament laws given to Israel and the present-day practice could hardly be more dramatic. In the Old Testament, loans to the poor were to be made at *zero* interest. Today in the West the poor pay *far higher* interest rates than anyone else! A biblical understanding of economic justice says that we must treat people appropriately, according to the norms and principles given by God – and that we must have an eye here for the economically weak. How have we in the twenty-first-century West come so far from that vision?

There are two key things to say here. The first is to note that high-cost credit, despite its deep problems, does seem to have a place in people's lives in the twenty-first century, for good or bad. I think we have to acknowledge the reality of this – even if the reality is extremely unsatisfactory. In May 2018 the FCA Chief Executive,

Andrew Bailey, gave a speech that included some important analysis. For example:

Credit is not the right option for all consumers. There is a group of consumers who are on such low or uncertain incomes or whose personal circumstances mean that any lending is likely to be inappropriate or unaffordable. Parts of the social welfare system are designed to provide assistance to them.[12]

But he then considered another group of consumers

who are on low incomes and may be financially vulnerable but are nonetheless able to sustain low repayments for small sums. However, the personal circumstances of these consumers can mean they are especially susceptible to unexpected changes to their income or expenditure demands, for example dealing with changes to their living arrangements at short notice.[13]

Bailey then noted that borrowing for these consumers is particularly costly, because of the risk of default – as we noted earlier. However, he then proceeded to say the following:

Our [the FCA's] view is that the provision of credit can nevertheless have a socially valuable function. High-cost credit users typically have low credit scores and many do not have savings but may need credit to make ends meet and avoid wider financial difficulties, for example, default on household bills or priority debts. They may also have very limited options for obtaining essential goods or for managing other larger purchases or bills. Consumers can benefit from using credit where repayments are sustainable and appropriate forbearance is shown if they have temporary repayment problems.[14]

It is hard to dispute the logic of this analysis. Despite its risks and expense, high-cost credit does seem to have a place in people's lives. And without access to such credit some people would face even greater difficulties, on occasions at least – such as having to manage for some period of time without key household appliances.

And yet we must balance this first point with a second: that 'market forces' will never provide a fully just and merciful outcome *in this sector*. The crucial thing to note here is that the Old Testament's provision of zero-interest loans was *not* based on commercial but on *compassionate* grounds. Here are the words from Deuteronomy 15:7–8:

> If anyone is poor among your fellow Israelites in any of the towns of the land that the LORD your God is giving you, do not be hard-hearted or tight-fisted towards them. Rather, be open-handed and freely lend them whatever they need.

That these loans to the poor were to be at zero interest is stated three times in the Old Testament (Deut. 23:19–20; Lev. 25:35–38; Exod. 22:25). In the book of Leviticus this zero-interest commandment is followed by a reminder of the plight of the Israelites as slaves in Egypt before their redeemer God came to their rescue:

> If any of your fellow Israelites become poor and are unable to support themselves among you, help them as you would a foreigner and stranger, so that they can continue to live among you. Do not take interest or any profit from them, but fear your God, so that they may continue to live among you. You must not lend them money at interest or sell them food at a profit. I am the LORD your God, who brought you out of Egypt to give you the land of Canaan and to be your God.
> (Lev. 25:35–38)

Again, then, we see that the purpose of the zero-interest loan was to *help* the person who had become poor; and the motivation includes that reminder of the people's own plight before the Lord in his compassion came to their rescue.

In chapter 4 we saw that our church communities today should apply the principle here of giving 'a hand up' to people who are poor and needy, wherever possible; there we were focusing on support for members of church communities, and in the local area in which any church community is located. But how can this radical and compassionate principle be applied to the low-income sector of the 'market' as a whole? Am I suggesting that profit-seeking financial institutions should make *compassionate* loans to those who are economically weak?

Well, *someone* should! That is the point. God's norms and principles have not changed. Justice in economic life, for any community, includes having a special concern for the poor and needy. Compassionate loans are part of this: they need not necessarily be at *zero* interest, but are given on the grounds of compassion, and low interest and zero interest can both fit that principle.

So market forces alone will not provide low-interest or zero-interest loans for the economically weak, which is plain from what we have seen already. What is needed, then, is some other way of operating. Here is exciting potential for *socially* driven enterprises, and some important examples of this, in the area of compassionate loans, certainly exist. In the UK and Republic of Ireland *credit unions* provide one such example. These are essentially saving-and-lending communities/clubs: members contribute savings (deposits), on which a below-market interest rate is paid, and are entitled to request low-interest loans.

A second example is given by microcredit (microfinance), especially in the Global South (Majority World): investors put deposits – again at below-market interest rates – into a microfinance institution (or bank), and these are then made available to people, on a 'hand up' basis, whose low income would never permit them access to normal market-based loans. As noted in chapter 4, a particularly successful case of this is the Grameen Bank based in Bangladesh, a microcredit institution committed to providing small amounts of working capital to the poor for self-employment.[15]

In the UK, however, the size of credit unions is far smaller than the demand for loans from people on low incomes. This is evident from the reality of how much *high-cost* credit is taken up. So enormous scope remains for socially driven alternative sources of credit for those on low incomes. The FCA readily acknowledges this.[16]

How would it be, then, if followers of Jesus Christ who are in positions of influence *within* the mainstream, and large banks and other financial institutions, were to encourage *these* financial institutions to set up, and/or invest in, alternative and *low*-cost credit sources? The motivation for this can never be profit: the grounds will be compassionate, not commercial. But the size of this low-income sector is relatively small, compared to the size of the mortgage sector, or other secured finance sector, or the property and commercial sector. So it is *not* a question of banks and others choosing a substantial reduction in profits. And that, in any case, would typically not be realistic – as we have seen in the previous chapter. But there is growing awareness of the responsibilities of large companies to a wider group of stakeholders and to wider society. So there is scope for followers of Christ, and indeed anyone, to start exploring initiatives here.

It is important to remember that these kinds of initiatives are *not* loss-making: they do not depend on the profits from other ventures subsidising losses on low-cost credit. Instead, the 'business model' comprises, crucially, deposits receiving *below*-market interest rates, together with low-cost small loans. In other words, it is the willingness of investors to devote funds on a social basis that provides the capital needed.

Low-cost credit and 'consumers'

I close this section with an important word of caution. When I quoted, earlier, the analysis offered by the FCA's Chief Executive, a significant word that he used several times was 'consumers'. For example, 'Consumers can benefit from using credit where repayments are sustainable and appropriate forbearance is shown if they have temporary repayment problems.' It is clearly an appropriate word to use, given the context of his analysis. However, the goal of the compassionate loans – to 'give a hand up' – discussed above is *not* to 'help consumers'. Instead, it is to help people in an economically weak position *to get into a stronger position*. The goal of this compassionate low-cost credit is *not* simply to enable people to purchase consumer goods, which they otherwise might not manage to obtain; rather, it is to help people move out of dependent poverty altogether.

Therefore, compassionate low-cost loans will really make sense for people in an economically weak position *only* when they comprise part of a wider package that will help that person's *income* to become greater and/or more reliable. This wider package may include, for example, help with developing skills, with job-seeking and with support – such as interview skills – for job applications and interviews. In the context of such a wide package a low-cost loan at a time of severe financial pressure could easily make good sense. But simply to assist someone through the next financial crisis, with no plan to avert future crises, is not providing any long-term 'hand up' help.

Given this emphasis on a wider package, it is clear that there must be a *personal* and *relational* dimension to low-cost compassionate loans. It will not be sufficient simply to have some automated application process devoid of advice and support of a personal nature.

In considering the very serious contemporary issues raised regarding high-cost credit for those most in need, this section has demonstrated the tremendous relevance of the biblical material on compassionate loans. Such loans can help to give people a 'hand up'. There is great potential for followers of Christ to use their influence in the finance arena to do justice and show mercy by means of this approach.

Greed, pride and folly in the arena of big finance

In April 2012 the then USA Treasury Secretary Timothy Geithner said, 'Most financial crises are caused by a mix of stupidity and greed and recklessness and risk-taking and hope.'[17]

In 2018, ten years after the demise of Lehman Brothers, which helped to trigger a massive financial crisis, Lucy O'Carroll (in 2008 an economist at one of the UK's largest financial institutions) wrote:

optimism bias in business creators is often positive. They need to have a substantial appetite for risk. And many of those businesses did survive – because they had successful products or services and because they hadn't taken on excessive debt.

But some of them went under, and some of that optimism could have simply been hubris: the excessive self-confidence that provokes the wrath of the gods in Greek tragedy. But the hubris at the big financial institutions went beyond what we saw with even our boldest clients.[18]

Many secular writers have commented on the central part that greed, hubris, pride and folly play in a financial crisis – especially the crisis that began in 2007–8. So this is not a line of argument offered only by Christians. But *why* can this kind of mindset be so prevalent in the world of corporate business, and particularly in the arena of finance? In chapter 5 I made a brief reference to the role that greed seems to play among some corporate executives – and not only in the finance arena. Now, in this final section of the current chapter I am going to devote a little more attention to the issue.

My aim here is not to preach a sermon against these attitudes. Instead, it is twofold: to help us understand more deeply what is going on here, in the light of the biblical witness, and how greed and pride can get in the way of *justice*; and, second, to help followers of Christ who are part of banks and other financial institutions to take greed, pride and folly into account as they seek to do justice in and through these institutions.

Definitions

Before going any further, we need to be clear in what we are talking about. By *greed* – especially regarding money and wealth – I mean excessive or unrestrained desire for *more*.[19] So there are two aspects to this: greed involves a very strong *desire* – an inner attitude and mindset; and a desire always to have *more*. In the context of the economy, money and wealth, greed means the unrestrained desire for more money and wealth. This definition fits closely with the way that the Bible talks about covetousness.[20]

By *pride* I mean conceit and vanity. And *hubris* – an even stronger form of pride – is a kind of arrogant pride (as in the quote above from O'Carroll, referring to the hubris of the gods in Greek tragedy). C. S. Lewis wrote:

> There is one vice of which no man in the world is free; which everyone in the world loathes when he sees it in someone else; and of which hardly any people, except Christians, ever imagine that they are guilty themselves . . . The vice I am talking of is Pride or Self-Conceit.[21]

As for *folly*, here I am using the word especially in its biblical sense, and particularly as found in the book of Proverbs. So folly is *not* a matter of low intelligence. Scholar Derek Kidner, in his commentary on Proverbs, wrote as follows, in relation to the word used most frequently for the 'fool':

> [the fool] has no idea of a patient search for wisdom: he has not the concentration for it . . . The root of his trouble is spiritual, not mental. He *likes* his folly . . . At bottom what he is rejecting is the fear of the Lord ['fear' in this context means 'godly awe'] . . . *In society* the fool is, in a word, a menace . . .[22]

Trying to understand greed, pride and folly

It seems to me that secular writers struggle to *understand* these mindsets, at least to any reasonable depth. 'Greed is so irrational!', people will say. 'It's stupid to be so proud!' And folly is, well, stupidity to the nth degree! But *why* are people 'irrational' and 'stupid' in these ways? What can explain this? After all, the people that get to the top of huge financial institutions do not get there by acting irrationally! One leading economist, Richard Layard, a Professor at the London School of Economics, has argued that, regarding the aspect of greed as *insatiable* (always desiring *more*), it is simply irrational and self-defeating.[23] And therefore, 'We should of course try to educate people away from both envy and greed, since neither is conducive to happiness.'[24]

But this approach is in danger of missing the point: Layard seems oddly confident in the power of education, in the face of decades and indeed millennia of economic greed. People *like* being greedy! People often *do* want to have more and more. This is the reality. They probably would not take kindly to the idea of being educated away from it.

Much the same could be said regarding pride, hubris and folly. Indeed, the quotation earlier from economist Lucy O'Carroll indicated that *some* kind of 'bias' in favour of optimism is probably essential for people who create businesses: who is to say, then, when 'optimism' becomes 'too much optimism'? Hindsight is a wonderful thing; but often it seems as though it is only *after* things become disastrous that someone can say, with hindsight, 'I acted out of pride there.'

The *biblical* understanding of greed, pride and folly goes much deeper. To start with, note how Jesus Christ *warns* against greed: 'Watch out! Be on your guard against all kinds of greed' (Luke 12:15). So greed – which can evidently come in 'all kinds' of ways – is dangerous, and we must guard against it. This is much more serious than being merely irrational. Jesus goes on to say, 'life does not consist in an abundance of possessions'. This is a stark warning to us.

The Bible is plain, also, in telling us the true nature of greed. In Colossians 3:5 the apostle Paul calls on his readers to 'put to death' whatever belongs to their earthly nature, and these, he writes, include 'greed, which is idolatry'. This is startling: greed is a form of *idolatry*. To be greedy is to worship a false god. This links very closely to what Jesus Christ stated in Matthew 6:24 about the love of Money (with a capital 'M' – translating, as noted earlier, a word that in the original is 'Mammon'): 'You cannot serve both God and Money' (Matt. 6:24). Money can be a rival to the one true God.

What, then, is the Bible's *explanation* for greed, pride (arrogance) and folly? From where do they come? Here again the teaching of Jesus Christ is plain. In Mark 7, for example, Jesus teaches his disciples about what defiles a human person, or makes someone unclean – that is, *morally* unclean. He is countering the idea that human sinfulness is merely external – something that comes in from the outside, or could be washed away or removed by washing with physical water. Jesus says:

> What comes out of a person is what defiles them. For it is from within, out of a person's heart, that evil thoughts come – sexual immorality, theft, murder, adultery, greed, malice, deceit, lewdness, envy, slander, arrogance and folly. All these evils come from inside and defile a person.
> (Mark 7:20–23)

Do you see that greed, arrogance and folly are on that list? It is from the *inside* that greed and all these other evils come. So greed, arrogance (pride) and folly are matters of the human heart: they are part of human sinfulness (see also Matt. 23:25; Luke 11:39).

The apostle Paul adds that greed and all other kinds of wickedness have come about as a result of humankind's rebellion against God (see Rom. 1:28–29). All of this is part of the *unrighteousness* of fallen, sinful human beings.[25]

The biblical explanation, then, is that greed, pride and folly lie deep inside the hearts of fallen and sinful human beings.

What has all of this to do with *economic justice*? A great deal. We have already seen that greed, arrogance and folly are linked in the Bible with other forms of wickedness and unrighteousness. But the closeness of the link between greed, arrogance and *injustice* is made even clearer by the Old Testament prophets. Consider, for example, these words from the prophet Micah:

> Woe to those who plan iniquity,
>   to those who plot evil on their beds!
> At morning's light they carry it out
>   because it is in their power to do it.
> They covet fields and seize them,
>   and houses, and take them.
> They defraud people of their homes,
>   they rob them of their inheritance.
> (Mic. 2:1–2)

The *behaviour* rebuked here includes iniquity, the seizing of other people's fields, and defrauding people of their homes. All of this is unjust. But the *motivation* is coveting: wanting more, and wanting what belongs to someone else. This is part of *greed*.

We hear something very similar from the prophet Jeremiah. Jeremiah addresses King Jehoiakim of Judah in 22:13–19.[26] He begins (v. 13) by saying:

> Woe to him who builds his palace by unrighteousness,
>> his upper rooms by injustice,
> making his own people work for nothing,
>> not paying them for their labour.

The economic injustice practised by this king is thus made clear at the outset. But the motivation Jehoiakim exhibits is greed: desire for more. This is made plain in the following verses. For example, the first half of verse 15 asks:

> Does it make you a king
>> to have more and more cedar?

Note that phrase 'more and more'; here the NIV 2011 translates a word that is translated elsewhere as 'competing'. Greed often has a competitive element: outdoing, 'doing better', than others. So we see that the element of pride is also clearly present. And it was wanting to be 'a king' – pride again – that drove Jehoiakim down this road of continuous acquisition.

The section concludes in verse 17 (having contrasted, in vv. 15–16, Jehoiakim with his father, King Josiah):

> But your eyes and your heart
>> are set only on dishonest gain,
> on shedding innocent blood
>> and on oppression and extortion.

So 'dishonest gain' – note again the strong sense of *greed* ('gaining') – goes along closely with *unrighteousness* and *injustice* (v. 13).

The Bible, then, draws close links between the inner attitudes (mindset) of greed, pride and folly and the outward behaviour of economic injustice.

Before we proceed to link all of this back to the large corporate institutions of today's world, we must hear clearly what God's ultimate solution is to all of the above ills. The amazing news that Jesus Christ announced is that he, the Son of God, had come to bring God's kingdom rule: a kingdom of justice, peace and joy (see Rom. 14:17). Despite all the *un*righteousness of humankind, God has stepped down and stepped in *for* us. This astonishing grace, totally undeserved by you and me, took Christ all the way to the cross of Calvary, where he took upon himself all the judgment and punishment that we justly deserved. Because of his death and resurrection, *new life* is available, for anyone: new creation, by the Holy Spirit of God. So God offers transformation from the inside out. Sins forgiven; the offer of being justified – declared just (righteous) in God's sight; new power for living in justice, peace and joy. All this and much more: all to be received simply, and solely, by faith – by looking to Jesus Christ and his death as the only ground for forgiveness, justification and salvation.

This is God's solution. Wherever he places us in his world we must be ready to share this glorious good news! Whether we are placed in a bank or a supermarket, in a lower position, humanly speaking, or a higher position, ultimately it is this gospel that is the power for salvation and transformation, for everyone who believes (Rom. 1:16).

Large financial institutions: the potential for doing justice despite greed and pride

Human nature has not changed since biblical times. In the twenty-first century the inner attitudes of greed, pride (hubris) and folly can still so easily take root – not least in huge corporations, and not least in the arena of big finance. We saw that at the beginning of this section. So when followers of Jesus Christ are called to work in, and be part of, these huge financial institutions, we must be realistic about looking out for signs of greed, pride and folly. There is potential for doing economic justice in and through these institutions, but the tendency towards these fallen (sinful) inner attitudes must be taken into account.

The same applies to the issues we looked at earlier in this chapter: the challenges to do with excessive lending, borrowing and debt, and the treatment of people who are economically weak. Followers of Christ involved in large financial institutions must be realistic regarding all of these, often enormous, challenges.

Even so, and as that realism is taken on board, there is still potential for doing economic justice in and through banks and financial institutions. A biblical understanding of economic justice applies at all levels and to all organizations.

For example, those who are in senior positions in these organizations must think and pray hard about how to use their influence for what is just. One aspect of this is for them to consider carefully, and practically, how to shape the *culture* of their institution. You may be in such a position yourself, or you may know others who are. It is clear that culture *comes from the top*. So the opportunity to mould the institutional culture is there: will we take that opportunity, or waste it?

The challenge of *culture* is certainly relevant when we take stock of the challenges posed by greed, pride and folly. In any organization such mindsets can easily take root, as I mentioned before. Those at the top need to examine their organization carefully in this regard, and then use their influence to remould the culture more in line with biblical economic justice.

This could mean, for example, assessing carefully any ways in which the institution has dealings with people who are economically weak. Given the huge scale of some banks and financial institutions, it is quite likely that they will have *some* dealings with the poor and needy – whether directly or more indirectly. In the case of Wonga – considered in the first main section of this chapter – one striking feature is that Wonga was backed by *high profile* investors.[27] There are many connections between companies across the world of business and finance. But biblical economic justice always calls us to have a special eye open for those who are economically weak.

And large organizations are in a position to have influence in many ways, whether directly or more indirectly.

I am *not* saying, by the way, that large-scale outside investors should simply withdraw funds from companies that are, or may be, acting with injustice; it is much more a question of senior executives inside such companies shaping positively a culture in which their company learns to value and practise more closely the principles and norms of economic justice.

Conclusion

This chapter has aimed to equip people with ways of thinking about some major challenges in the arena of finance – especially regarding economic justice. I have given a few suggestions along the way of how these ways of thinking might begin to work out in practice. But this book can never claim to be a 'manual' or detailed guide: the Bible gives us much teaching on economic justice. The challenge to study and then put it into practice, in the finance arena, must ultimately be met by those who have influence in that arena.

7

Wider society: nationally and globally

The prophet Amos said:

Take away from me the noise of your songs;
   to the melody of your harps I will not listen.
But let justice roll down like waters,
   and righteousness like an ever-flowing stream.
(Amos 5:23–24 ESVUK)

Introduction

What will it mean to do economic justice in society as a whole? In this book we have been looking at economic justice in our own relationships – as consumers, in the workplace, in church communities – and then (continuing to move out in a series of concentric circles) in and through firms, companies and large banks and other financial institutions. In this chapter we move out further and consider economic justice in society as a whole – both nationally and globally. In all this I am continuing to show especially how the Bible has much to say about doing justice in economic life.

There are some crucial and controversial issues to address here. For example, is there too much inequality of income and wealth in our economy and across the world? Should we be concerned only about *absolute* poverty, or *relative* poverty as well? What role should governments ('the state') play in trying to bring about greater economic justice? What about other (*non*-governmental) social institutions (e.g. charities, community groups, schools, social

143

enterprises, trades unions): how can we do economic justice in and through them? When we look at the world overall, what about *globalization*? Is this helping to bring more justice, or more injustice? In all of those dimensions and institutions, in what ways can followers of Christ be working for economic justice?

Acknowledge that some questions here are controversial

A first step is to be honest about the controversial nature of some of these issues. If you run a radio chat show, try making the following question the topic of a phone-in debate: 'Is there too much inequality of income and wealth?' You can be sure of a lively debate!

This kind of question is controversial both among Christians and in wider society. Across the left–right political spectrum, people hold very different views on such issues, and often hold them very deeply and passionately. The clashes between left and right can be fierce. Some Christians see themselves as being, politically, on the left: 'God made all human beings equal: the inequalities of income and wealth today are terrible and wrong.' Other disciples of Christ view themselves as being on the right: 'The equality that matters is equality of *opportunity*: to attempt to improve one's situation in life.'[1] People of this persuasion will typically suggest that some level of economic inequality is unavoidable, and will argue that to try to enforce equality, or simply *greater* equality, is unlikely to be effective in practice – and in any case owes more to Karl Marx than to the Bible.

So, opposite views are held, and held with passion. Controversy abounds.

The same applies to issues regarding how much of a role the state should play in economic and social life, and especially in bringing about a greater degree of economic justice. Put to one side for a moment the question of whether or not people from the left and right can agree on what 'economic justice' is. Left-wingers – Christians and more generally – are typically in favour of greater governmental intervention, and despair at people who say 'free markets are best'; right-wingers are much more suspicious of such state-led action, arguing that it is either a dangerous restriction on individual freedom, or likely to be wasteful and ineffective, or both.

Controversy is also rife when it comes to questions about poverty. Not about *absolute* material poverty: at every point along the left–right spectrum it is agreed that absolute poverty cannot be accepted and should be combatted, in one way or another. But where people disagree is about *relative* poverty; that is, poverty defined in terms of how much income a person, or household, has in relation to some kind of measure of *average* income. Issues about equality and relative poverty are closely connected, since the less relative poverty there is, typically the greater equality there will be.

So it is important to acknowledge that these issues are controversial. It would be foolish to ignore this. It is, therefore, with a degree of trepidation that I enter this territory!

Controversies linked to trends

The controversies about poverty, inequality and equality relate to what is happening in countries such as the UK, and indeed across the world. These debates are not about 'abstract ideology' or simply about *ideas*.

With regard to the number of people across the world who are living in extreme poverty, figures produced by the World Bank in September 2018 say that 736 million people were living on less than $1.90 a day.[2] This is an enormous number of people: no less than 10% of the world's population.[3] We can be thankful that this is an improvement on previous years. In the words of the World Bank Group President, Jim Yong Kim, in September 2018, quoted in the same press release: 'Over the last 25 years, more than a billion people have lifted themselves out of extreme poverty, and the global poverty rate is now lower than it has ever been in recorded history.' But 736 million is still a colossal number, and we must not let up in our efforts here. Biblical economic justice requires a special concern for the poor and needy.

The trends regarding inequality and equality have generated increasing concern in recent years. Extremely influential here has been a book published by Thomas Piketty, a French economist. The English-language version was published in 2014.[4] The book is, among other things, a detailed study of economic data on income, wealth and returns to capital, over more than a century – up until 2012. Piketty shows that since 1980 there have been major increases in inequality, both in income and wealth, especially in certain countries.

In the USA, as Piketty demonstrates, there has recently been a quite rapid doubling in the proportion of income earned by the top 1% of people. (By the 'top' 1% I mean simply those who earn the most.) Out of income for the whole USA population, the proportion earned by the top 1% increased from about 8% in 1980 to 17% in 2012. In other words, over a period of only thirty-three years the richest not only became richer, but their *share* of total income more than doubled.[5]

In the UK the Commission on Economic Justice (CEJ) in its final report (published in 2018) expressed grave concern about inequality of income and wealth. They pointed out some key facts, including

a long-term decline in the share of national income which has gone to wages and salaries. In the mid-1970s the Bank of England calculates that the 'labour share' of national income was almost 70 per cent; today it is around 55 per cent . . . The other side of this coin has been the rising share of income going to the owners of capital, as the returns on financial and real estate assets have consistently outpaced the rate of economic growth.[6]

The CEJ linked this concern to deeper trends in inequality in the UK:

In recent years our economy has been growing, but most people are no better off than a decade ago . . . Over the last 40 years, only 10 per cent of national income growth went to the bottom half of the income distribution, while almost two-fifths went to the richest 10 per cent. The UK is the fifth most unequal country in Europe in terms of income, while inequality of wealth is even greater: 44 per cent of wealth is owned by just 10 per cent of the population. The huge growth in property values means that today's young people, many of them priced out of the housing market, are set to be poorer than their parents. The UK is Europe's most geographically unbalanced economy, with wide disparities between the nations and regions, and many once-thriving communities suffering economic decline.[7]

If we look carefully at the picture described here by the CEJ, we see two distinct, though related, trends. One is that some people and regions are no better off, and some worse off, than decades earlier. This is a comparison of income *over time*. The second trend highlighted is greater inequality, at least of wealth, which involves a comparison *between people* or population groups. It is important to note that these two things are not the same.

To the picture painted by the CEJ we could add the idea of *cycles of deprivation*. Such a cycle is where people, households, communities or regions are, for whatever reason, trapped in a cycle of poverty and/or very low income. Whereas some other people and groups experience a growth in income over time, these people are somehow stuck in a cycle of deprivation. Imagine, for example, a town in north-east England where the previously flourishing steel industry collapsed several years ago. Since then incomes have fallen, and other local industries have declined due to shrinking local demand for what they produce; that in turn has led to some school teachers moving away – perhaps because their spouse or partner has become unemployed, and they as a household can no longer make ends meet in that locality. That then leads to a decline in the quality of education. And so the next generation is also affected.

To that bleak picture one could add that the local government might also suffer a decline in income – due to a fall in income from business rates, as businesses shut down, and from council tax, as people move away. Therefore, the quality of provision of local services also declines. This only makes matters worse across the region. This is what is meant by a 'cycle of deprivation'.

I will come back shortly to these recent trends in income and inequality, as highlighted by, for example, the CEJ. But for now it is important to acknowledge what has been happening, and to be honest about the deep and controversial questions about inequality, equality and poverty, and about the role of the state in trying to bring about greater economic justice.

What kinds of answers are given by a biblical approach to economic justice?

I am convinced that a biblical understanding of economic justice is relevant to the controversial questions relating to inequality and poverty. However, I want to show that it does *not* give us a precise set of answers to these questions. It does present us with some powerful principles, and these are of great relevance in the twenty-first century. But it does *not* provide answers to questions about the role of government, or about whether or not there is too much inequality.

Am I ducking the issues? No! Let me try to show you why.

As we saw earlier, doing economic justice biblically means treating people appropriately, according to the norms and principles given by God; it requires a special concern for people who are poor, needy and economically weak; it emphasizes the quality of relationships – notably one-to-one relationships; and it means that everyone participates in God's blessings, including material blessings. These four elements provide powerful and relevant principles for today. But, as you may have noticed, these four elements say *nothing at all* about the role of the state (government). This, I would argue, is no accident. God's call to us to do economic justice is based upon his own character – he is the God who *loves justice*. And the call to do justice is to all people. Therefore it is not intrinsic to doing economic justice that the state must have a part to play.

Please do not misunderstand me here. I am *not* arguing for a 'libertarian' position, in which the state has as small a role as possible. I am simply saying that the Bible gives us no grounds for saying that the state *must* have an intrinsic role in doing economic justice. This is an important point to make, because in the current climate in the West there is often a tendency to assume that, ultimately, it is somehow for the government to ensure justice in economic life. According to the Bible, however, the call to do economic justice rests on the shoulders of everyone in society.

Consider Abraham, for example. On the very first occasion in the Bible when the words 'justice and righteousness' occur together, look at what is said by Yahweh, the LORD, regarding Abraham:

> For I have chosen him, that he may command his children and his household after him to keep the way of the LORD by doing righteousness and justice, so that the LORD may bring to Abraham what he has promised him.
> (Gen. 18:19 ESVUK)

Abraham had a responsibility to do righteousness and justice – and that included his economic dealings. He could not delegate responsibility for doing economic justice to the government or king.

Consider, similarly, what God said through Moses to the people of Israel as they were about to go into the land promised to them (Canaan). In Deuteronomy 4 Moses says that the people must 'hear the decrees and laws I am about to teach you' (v. 1). He proceeds to predict (vv. 6–8) how the people in other nations will respond when, or if, the people of Israel observe carefully all these laws. One of the things that the Israelites will then be able to say is that the decrees and laws given to them (Israel) are *righteous*. And, as we have seen at various places in this book, *righteousness* and *justice* are closely related in the Old Testament. It is worth reading verses 6–8 in full:

> Observe them carefully, for this will show your wisdom and understanding to the nations, who will hear about all these decrees and say, 'Surely this great nation is a wise and understanding people.' What other nation is so great as to have their gods near them the way the LORD our God is near us whenever

we pray to him? And what other nation is so great as to have such righteous decrees and laws as this body of laws I am setting before you today?

So *everyone* had to obey the wise and righteous laws given by God. Justice and righteousness could not be delegated to the governing authorities.

How does all this apply to the twenty-first century? Some countries have a relatively larger role for government, including in economic activity. One simple measure for this is the amount of government spending on goods and services, as a proportion of a country's GDP. Other countries have a relatively smaller role for the state in the economy. My argument is in two parts: first, that the principles of economic justice apply in *all* of these countries; second, that however large or small a role the state plays, responsibility for doing economic justice rests on the shoulders of everybody in each country – it cannot simply be passed on to the state.

I will come back in a later section and say a bit more about the responsibilities of a nation's leaders in doing economic justice. But the point here can be summed up like this: the Bible does not provide us with a precise set of social and economic arrangements, or directions, about how much of a role the state should play in doing economic justice, that apply to all countries over all time; and the Bible does not delegate economic justice to the government – instead, everyone has responsibility for doing economic justice.

To put this another way: the principles of biblical economic justice can be applied all the way across the left–right political spectrum; that is, in countries that have a greater role for the government in economic life, and in those that have a lesser role for it.[8] But in no case can all responsibility for doing economic justice be delegated to the government.

What about the controversial questions regarding inequality, equality and poverty? The same kind of basic answer has to be given: the Bible simply does not provide us with a precise set of social and economic arrangements that apply to all countries over all time. For example, it does not specify tax rates, or sets of measures for how to equip people with skills for the workplace, or precise arrangements for the level of social security payments that should be available to people. The biblical teaching does not mandate any numerical or statistical amount of inequality that is permissible; and it does not require that each person or household in a country should have precisely the same (identical) amount of income and/or wealth.

Instead, the biblical teaching gives the key elements of what doing economic justice means. It gives us principles for how people should treat one another in economic relationships. And it tells us that everyone is to participate in God's blessings, including material blessings. But if someone wants something more precise than all of that, they will have to look somewhere other than the Scriptures.

Everyone should participate in God's blessings: but that is *not* the same thing as equality

Some readers may now be asking, 'You claimed that the Bible is relevant to the controversial questions relating to inequality and poverty. But you have now argued that the biblical material operates at the broader level of *principles*, rather than offering *precise* guidance. Make up your mind! Either the Bible addresses these issues or it does not!'

That is a fair challenge, and so I now want to say more about biblical economic justice in relation to inequality and poverty. And I want to argue that the emphasis on *everyone participating in God's blessings* takes us in a somewhat different direction from that of a focus on inequality and equality.

Back in chapter 1 we saw from the Old Testament this emphasis on everyone participating in God's blessings, including material blessings. I showed the significance of the third-year tithe, enabling those *without* land to eat and be satisfied. This emphasis was re-inforced, for Old Testament Israel, by a range of other provisions; for example, compassionate loans for the needy; provision of housing and work for people who fall on hard times (e.g. Lev. 25:39–43);

the *gleaning* principle (e.g. Lev. 19:9–10); and the promise of a grand returning of land, every fifty years – in the year of Jubilee – to the family group to which it had originally been entrusted (Lev. 25).

It is all very well to put this in terms of a *principle*: 'everyone sharing in God's blessings, including material blessings'. But is that not a bit *abstract*? What does that look like in reality? We must take a closer look at what was to happen in the Jubilee (fiftieth) year. Here are the instructions given by God through Moses:

> Count seven sabbath years – seven times seven years – so that the seven sabbath years amount to a period of forty-nine years. Then sound the trumpet everywhere on the tenth day of the seventh month; on the Day of Atonement sound the trumpet throughout your land. Consecrate the fiftieth year and proclaim liberty throughout the land to all its inhabitants. It shall be a jubilee for you; each of you is to return to your family property and to your own clan. The fiftieth year shall be a jubilee for you; do not sow and do not reap what grows of itself or harvest the untended vines. For it is a jubilee and is to be holy for you; eat only what is taken directly from the fields.
>
> In this Year of Jubilee everyone is to return to their own property.
> (Lev. 25:8–13)

This is a radical requirement. Imagine you are playing a game of *Monopoly* – a version where everyone starts the game by being dealt properties of a roughly similar value, as well as some cash. As the game proceeds – not unlike the 'game' of economic life – some players gain more properties, while others lose. After you have been playing for, perhaps, an hour, there is a clear winner. But then, suddenly, it is announced, 'Each player is to return to the properties he or she owned at the start.' If you have been doing well, this announcement is bad news! If you have lost properties, then clearly it is good news!

We need to be aware of a few things here in order to understand this teaching from the Old Testament. First, the people of Israel comprised both *families* and *clans*: the family was the household, typically comprising more people than the 'nuclear' family that has become more common in Western countries in more recent times; the *clan* was a wider 'kinship' group – people in the clan were still related by blood to one another, and had some shared ancestry. Families and clans were in turn also part of a *tribe*, as in the twelve tribes of Israel. Second, when the people of Israel entered the land (Canaan) promised to them by God, the land was allocated on a roughly equal basis (see Num. 33:54) and on a detailed basis, clan by clan. (You can read details in the book of Joshua, e.g. chs. 13 – 19.) Third, in the agrarian setting of the Old Testament, *land* was a key economic resource. Land provided work, income, food and stability. The equivalent to the role that land played in an Old Testament setting in a Western twenty-first-century economy would be some combination of education and skills, 'human capital', with perhaps some ownership stake in businesses/corporations ('financial capital'). For in our setting it is *these* things that help to provide work, income, food and economic stability. I will come back later to possible ways forward regarding these 'capital' stakes.

So what would happen in the Jubilee year (and, unlike our *Monopoly* game earlier, it would *not* come as a surprise announcement) is that each family and clan would return to the property (land) that had been allocated way back in the days of Joshua. In other words, once every generation or so – every fifty years – there was a 'reset', enabling every household and clan to have a stake once again in economic life.

This stake in economic life, based on the Old Testament teaching, is termed an 'equity' stake by Michael Rhodes and his co-authors in their 2018 book.[9] And they helpfully link this equity principle with the other related Old Testament teachings – as I did earlier in this chapter:

All the charity and assistance in Israel's laws occurred in the shadow of the Jubilee. Israelites gleaned in the fields of others in the sure hope that they would be restored to the fields of their fathers. It was not enough for every Israelite to have access to work; when Yahweh was on the throne, every Israelite had equity in the economy.[10]

Equity is not the same thing as *equality*. An equity stake in this context means an ownership stake; or, since in the Old Testament it was recognized that God is the owner, and human beings only trustees or stewards, then we might say this is a *trusteeship stake*. This equity stake provides people with a solid economic foundation upon which they can flourish and earn a living, with protection in law from others who might try to seize it from them. That is the purpose of this equity stake. The fundamental principle is not to do with equality – everyone having the same – but with everyone having a stable foundation for economic life and flourishing.

Clearly, there was *some* element of equality in this provision of an equity stake; as we have seen, land was initially allocated so that every clan had roughly the same amount (see Num. 33:54), but it would be incorrect to say either that 'equality' was the driving force or that this whole set of provisions could be adequately summed up under the simple heading of 'equality'.

Before linking all this to the present-day controversies regarding inequality, it is important to recognize that it is in Jesus Christ that these laws from the Old Testament have their ultimate fulfilment. Jesus taught plainly that he had not come to abolish the Law or the Prophets 'but to fulfil them' (Matt. 5:17). Rhodes and his fellow authors, in summarizing the 'equity' principle, go on to show something of the way in which the Jubilee provision was fulfilled by Christ:

Scripture shows us that in God's economy, everyone has a stake in the community. The Israelites were introduced to this economy in the wilderness, and God gave them laws like the Jubilee to establish and protect that economy when they entered the promised land. When Jesus came on the scene, he adapted the Jubilee as a metaphor of the physical, social, spiritual, and economic liberation that he came to announce [see Luke 4:14–21] in his own life, death, and resurrection.[11]

Having reviewed all of this biblical material, how does it connect with today's controversies regarding inequality and poverty? The principle that everyone should participate in God's blessings includes, as we have been seeing, a strong commitment to everyone having a meaningful stake in the economic life of the community. This may sound a bit like seeking some measure of equality, or some reduction in inequality. But inequality and equality are only *measures* of something: they describe only a state of affairs; in themselves they do not offer a vision.[12] The vision of economic justice given in the Bible is much more far-reaching than a mere state of affairs: it is that everyone can work and flourish, under God's good hand, and can enjoy his blessings – including material blessings – in stability, and all to his praise and glory. And in that vision what matters is not some numerical measure of equality, but that each individual and household has a meaningful stake and is flourishing.

How about issues concerning relative poverty? Well, we in twenty-first-century economies may be wise to take note of statistics about relative poverty – because they shed some light on groups of people who are *not* flourishing; and we will want to find ways to enable these people to be able to have a meaningful stake in economic life. But the extent of relative poverty *in itself* will not be the prime concern. Instead, the driving force, according to biblical economic justice, is to enable people to have training, skills, work and, in due course, a capital stake that will enable them to participate in God's blessings and flourish.

So we have seen that the biblical material on economic justice links in powerful ways to some of today's key issues and controversial questions. Having done that, we now turn to explore at a more practical level how a biblical understanding of economic justice can be applied in today's societies and economies.

And the first task here is, as I promised earlier, to say more about the responsibilities of a nation's leaders in doing economic justice.

The role of governments in doing economic justice

Earlier in this chapter I argued that, according to the Bible, all people in a society have a responsibility to do economic justice: this cannot be delegated to the government. Economic justice involves people treating one another appropriately, according to the norms and principles given by God, and each of us has a responsibility in this, irrespective of any role for the state or government. Nevertheless, it may well be in practice that national leaders and governments should play a useful part. In this section we will first look in more detail at the biblical material on the role of those in national authority in doing economic justice. Then we will explore how all of that can apply in our setting today.

In the Old Testament the unfolding of God's revelation of himself and the history of the people of Israel are intertwined. This is particularly striking when it comes to the role of national and community leaders, not least in relation to economic justice. When God gave his laws to the Israelites through Moses, the people had no human king. In this way they were unlike many of the surrounding nations. But there were still national leaders, of whom Moses was an outstanding example. The Old Testament laws regarding justice in economic life clearly envisaged some role for *leaders* in upholding the laws, in making judicial decisions as necessary, and hence in economic justice. One early example of this is seen in Exodus 18 – *before* God gave his laws to Moses at Mount Sinai: Moses came to realize that there were far too many difficult cases for him alone to deal with, so he chose leaders and officials to make good judgments (vv. 24–26). No doubt some of these cases would involve matters of economic life; for example, disputes about who was to farm which piece of land, and who owned which cattle.

The same practice of appointing leaders and judges was then commanded by God as part of his giving of the Law through Moses. In Deuteronomy 16:18–20 we read:

> Appoint judges and officials for each of your tribes in every town the LORD your God is giving you, and they shall judge the people fairly. Do not pervert justice or show partiality. Do not accept a bribe, for a bribe blinds the eyes of the wise and twists the words of the innocent. Follow justice and justice alone, so that you may live and possess the land the LORD your God is giving you.

The strong emphasis on *justice* is striking. The Hebrew word for justice is *mišpāṭ*, which, as we saw in earlier chapters, has much relevance in the Old Testament to economic life. A key role for these leaders and officials, then, was to *uphold* the just laws as given by God. In this we see again that doing economic justice was a responsibility on all the people. A key role for community and national leaders – in relation to *economic* life – would be to act as necessary in cases where there was dispute, or breaking of laws, or some ambiguity.

A helpful example of this kind of action on the part of community leaders is given in the book of Ruth. By this time in their history the people of Israel were living in the promised land, and leadership of the nation as a whole was provided by a series of individuals termed *judges* (see Ruth 1:1). Ruth was a woman from Moab, a neighbouring country. She and another Moabite woman, Orpah, had each married Israelite men, who were brothers; the mother of these men, also an Israelite, was Naomi. Naomi was married to Elimelech. Tragically, all three husbands died. Ruth decided that instead of returning to her home country she would stay with Naomi, her mother-in-law, in the land of Israel. *However*, Naomi and Ruth were in a very weak position, economically, as widows. In that socio-cultural setting ownership of land rested with the male heir. If the man died, possession would pass to another man in the wider family or clan – see below.

We then read (2:1–3) how Ruth went gleaning in the fields – as the Law entitled her to. We looked at this Old Testament gleaning principle earlier, in chapter 1. It turned out that Ruth was working in a field that belonged to a man named Boaz, who was from the same clan as Naomi. To cut a longish story short – which includes a wonderful love story between Boaz and Ruth, although with a fair degree of tension – Boaz decided that he would be pleased to acquire a piece of land that had belonged to Naomi's husband, now deceased. It is a fair guess that he had his eyes, romantically, on Ruth as well. However, there was another man who was a closer relative to Naomi than Boaz was. This man had first claim: he was entitled to acquire ('redeem' – buy back) this piece of land. What was to be done?

This is where the local community leaders (elders) came in, which illustrates their role in aspects of economic justice. In Ruth 4 we read that Boaz went up to 'the town gate' – the place where the local court/elders would meet – and met with this other man (the nearer relative of Naomi). Boaz took ten of the elders, and in their presence addressed this other man ('the kinsman-redeemer' or 'redeemer'). A brief conversation then followed. It is worth hearing their words in full:

> Then he [Boaz] said to the redeemer, 'Naomi, who has come back from the country of Moab, is selling the parcel of land that belonged to our relative Elimelech. So I thought I would tell you of it and say, "Buy it in the presence of those sitting here and in the presence of the elders of my people." If you will redeem it, redeem it. But if you will not, tell me, that I may know, for there is no one besides you to redeem it, and I come after you.'
>
> And he said, 'I will redeem it.'
>
> Then Boaz said, 'The day you buy the field from the hand of Naomi, you also acquire Ruth the Moabite, the widow of the dead, in order to perpetuate the name of the dead in his inheritance.' Then the redeemer said, 'I cannot redeem it for myself, lest I impair my own inheritance. Take my right of redemption yourself, for I cannot redeem it.'
> (Ruth 4:3–6 ESVUK)

It was then agreed that Boaz would buy the land, and all of this was witnessed by the ten elders. These men ensured that economic justice was done. (And Boaz did marry Ruth, by the way!)

Another example of a community leader who did economic justice is Job. In Job 29 he gives a powerful account of the ways in which he typically acted at 'the gate of the city'. For example:

> I rescued the poor who cried for help,
> and the fatherless who had none to assist them.
> (v. 12)

And 'I was a father to the needy' (v. 16).

Some years after the time of Ruth and Boaz the people of Israel decided that they wanted to have a *king*: we read about this in 1 Samuel 8. This request displeased God, because it indicated that they were ultimately rejecting not only God's chosen leaders/judges – such as Samuel – but God himself. Even so, God in his sovereign purposes chose to accede to the people's request. As we will see in a moment, an important role in *doing economic justice* would be given by God to the king.

Back in the book of Deuteronomy we read that God foresaw that, centuries later, the people would desire to have a king, and thus be like the surrounding nations (Deut. 17:14). In acceding to this request, God makes it very plain that the king – and succeeding kings – must read and follow all the words of God's law (Deut. 17:18–20). This would of course include everything to do with economic justice. Obeying and upholding the law of God was a major responsibility laid on the kings of Israel, within the covenant relationship between God and his people – as many of the narrative books of the Old Testament make plain.

Israel's first king was Saul. After his death, David became king. (Generations later, one of David's descendants was born in Bethlehem: Jesus – 'great David's Greater Son'.) And after David died, Solomon, one of his sons, became king. In this next phase of Israel's history we see that, under God, the king was to have important responsibilities with regard to economic justice.

A clear statement of this is in Psalm 72, which has the heading 'Of Solomon'. Consider Psalm 72:1–4:

> Endow the king with your justice, O God,
>   the royal son with your righteousness.
> May he judge your people in righteousness,
>   your afflicted ones with justice.
>
> May the mountains bring prosperity to the people,
>   the hills the fruit of righteousness.
> May he defend the afflicted among the people
>   and save the children of the needy;
>   may he crush the oppressor.

There is a very clear economic dimension here: 'prosperity' and 'fruit' unmistakeably involve material and economic aspects; and in economic dealings there is always, in a fallen, sinful world, the possibility that some people will be badly treated, 'afflicted' and oppressed. And so this psalm is a prayer for the king to be endowed richly with *justice* and *righteousness*: positively, with the resultant blessing in economic prosperity; but also in defending the afflicted and crushing the oppressor.

We see a similar emphasis in the book of the prophet Jeremiah, who lived several generations later. Consider what God says to, and then through, him:

> This is what the LORD says: 'Go down to the palace of the king of Judah and proclaim this message there: "Hear the word of the LORD to you, king of Judah, you who sit on David's throne – you, your officials and your people who come through these gates. This is what the LORD says: do what is just and right. Rescue from the hand of the oppressor the one who has been robbed. Do no wrong or violence to the foreigner, the fatherless or the widow, and do not shed innocent blood in this place. For if you are careful to carry out these commands, then kings who sit on David's throne will come through the

gates of this palace, riding in chariots and on horses, accompanied by their officials and their people. But if you do not obey these commands, declares the LORD, I swear by myself that this palace will become a ruin."'

(Jer. 22:1–5)

Again, the responsibilities upon the king include a clear requirement to rescue those who have been robbed economically, and to do what is just.[13]

Let me give one more example, from that same chapter in Jeremiah. (We looked at this in more detail in chapters 1 and 6.) Here the requirements upon the king – especially regarding economic justice – are seen by the *contrast* between King Jehoiakim, to whom Jeremiah is speaking, and his father, King Josiah:

'Does it make you a king
    to have more and more cedar?
Did not your father have food and drink?
    He did what was right and just,
    so all went well with him.
He defended the cause of the poor and needy,
    and so all went well.
Is that not what it means to know me?'
    declares the LORD.
'But your eyes and your heart
    are set only on dishonest gain,
on shedding innocent blood
    and on oppression and extortion.'

(Jer. 22:15–17)

The failure and wickedness of successive kings of Israel – described in both the narrative and prophetic books of the Old Testament – is a disturbing story. They did *not* do economic justice. But the Bible does not end the story there. In the Old Testament we read prophecies of a future king who *will* act in perfect righteousness – one such prophecy comes in the very next chapter in Jeremiah,

23:5–6 – and who will indeed redeem from all sin those who look to him. In Isaiah 11:1 we read of a shoot who 'will come up from the stump of Jesse' – Jesse was King David's father – on whom the Spirit of the Lord will rest (v. 2). And concerning this king, whom the New Testament reveals to be Jesus Christ, the prophecy continues:

> and he will delight in the fear of the LORD.
>
> He will not judge by what he sees with his eyes,
>   or decide by what he hears with his ears;
> but with righteousness he will judge the needy,
>   with justice he will give decisions for the poor of the earth.
> He will strike the earth with the rod of his mouth;
>   with the breath of his lips he will slay the wicked.
> Righteousness will be his belt
>   and faithfulness the sash round his waist.
> (vv. 3–5)

What a wonderful king! This king, Jesus Christ, calls his followers to seek first the kingdom of God and his righteousness (Matt. 6:33). In looking at what the Old Testament teaches about the role of national leaders and kings in doing economic justice, it is very important that we see all of that in the light of Jesus Christ.

To summarize what we have been looking at in the Old Testament: in the context of Old Testament Israel, the national and community leaders – and especially the king – were to play an important part in doing economic justice. They were to uphold God's laws, which set out, among other things, the responsibilities on *all* the people for doing justice. They were themselves to do what is just. They were to defend the cause of the poor and needy and to crush oppressive economic behaviour.

Application to our twenty-first-century setting

To apply biblical material from its own context to *our* context must always be done with care. Throughout this book I have been arguing that we can validly derive from the Scriptures *principles* for economic behaviour and economic justice; and it is these principles that we should apply in today's setting. This same approach is relevant for the Old Testament material regarding the role of national and community leaders in doing economic justice. It seems to me valid to give the following principles. First, there is a role for those in authority to uphold laws that reflect the moral teachings of the Bible, including in relation to economic life. (In practice, in today's secular setting leaders may or may not see this role as upholding moral values *that derive ultimately from the word of God*; but in reality God is the only source of true ethical values.)

Second, there is a role for those in authority to focus on those who are economically weak – 'the poor and needy', in typical Old Testament language: and this includes working to enable those who are economically weak to *flourish*. For, as we have seen, much of the thrust of the Old Testament teaching is to ensure that the poor and needy are given 'a hand up', with the result that everyone participates in God's blessings, including material blessings.

Third, those in authority must act where there is economic oppression. Such oppression can include use of economic power to mistreat people; for example, in unjust weights and measures, in abuse of the legal system to remove from people that which is rightfully theirs (such as land); in oppressive treatment of employees, and similarly of suppliers and consumers.

Clearly, all of this is potentially far-reaching – especially the matters covered under that third point. How far this should be taken, however, is something on which I think we must be cautious. As I argued earlier, the Bible does *not* mandate any precise set of social and economic arrangements. Therefore it seems to me a matter of using sensible reasoning, guided by all of what the Bible teaches. We must not overclaim. How we put into practice the kinds of principles I have sketched out above is up to us, but we must not claim biblical approval for whatever proposals we put forward.

The Old Testament language of 'oppression' – a strong word – suggests that it is especially the *excessive* abuses of economic power where the authorities should take action. Certainly, that is my direction of thinking. There are clear warnings in the Bible about the dangers of 'overcentralizing' power; for example, in the same section in Deuteronomy in which God first says that he will permit Israel to have a king: see Deuteronomy 17:16–17. We would be wise not to give too much economic power to *any* institution – whether private or public sector.

However, the reality of today's business world is that there are some extremely large private sector corporations and companies; and these – in a fallen, sinful world – always have the potential to abuse their power in ways that would be very harmful to many people. In these circumstances it may be that one of the best ways to help prevent that from happening is for there to be another powerful body to keep them in check; and the only alternative power base with sufficient size, and any kind of legitimacy, is probably that of a national government – or even a partnership between a number of national governments.

Ideas along those lines take us into a related area where national authorities and governments might seek to work for greater economic justice, namely *regulation* of economic activity.

A role for the authorities in economic regulation?

Markets for goods and services have many advantages. Most economists acknowledge this. We saw something of this in an earlier chapter, where we looked at the insights of the great philosopher and economist Adam Smith. But most economists would also acknowledge 'market failure', which refers to what happens if a market – for example, the market for domestic energy – fails to allocate resources efficiently. For example, at the prices charged by the suppliers, demand and supply do not equal one another. Or the prices charged are thought to be excessively high, with the result that output may be lower than thought desirable. Market failure can occur due to a variety of reasons, such as monopoly power: there is only one main producer (supplier), which uses its power to raise prices to a level that is exploitative.

Another cause of market failure is what economists term 'negative externalities'. An example here is the emissions of carbon dioxide

(CO_2): the production of one product (e.g. oil refining) involves outcomes that are harmful to people directly involved in that market, while others who suffer (e.g. air pollution) have no way of forcing the producer to compensate them, or indeed to curtail production.

In situations of market failure there is a strong argument that the public authorities should step in to try to mitigate the failure. In other words, there is a strong case for *regulation*.

This book is not the place for a detailed assessment of the many questions raised in relation to market failure and regulation. But it is important to see that one aspect of market failure is the potential for some people or companies to act *unjustly*. Abuse of monopoly power is one clear example of that. It seems sensible, therefore, that the authorities should be willing to act to regulate markets, especially where it is likely that clear economic injustice is otherwise likely to keep recurring. Such an approach fits quite well with the general argument of the last few pages: national and local leaders do have a role, in a fallen world, in acting on behalf of the poor and needy, and in combatting oppressive economic behaviour.

The role of non-governmental social institutions in doing economic justice

In this chapter we are looking at how we do economic justice in wider society. It has been necessary to spend quite a bit of time on the role of national leaders and governments, because there are some important – and contentious – issues there. But, as I have been arguing, economic justice must not be delegated to the government: the requirement to do economic justice rests on everybody. Therefore it is also important to devote some space to looking at the role of non-governmental social institutions. These include charities, community groups, trades unions, schools and social enterprises. This section is relatively short – partly because I do not think there are many contentious issues here. Even though this section is briefer, the scope here is very important: there is tremendous opportunity for us to do economic justice in and through these other social institutions.

Our local church community has a close link with mission partners David and his wife Priti, who live and work in Bangladesh. They are Christians who have started up a business that aims, among other things, to provide paid work and a stable income for some of the poorest people in Bangladesh. This company produces coffins, potentially for sale anywhere in the world. You could describe this as a 'social enterprise' and refer to it under the heading of 'business as mission'.

Whatever the terminology, this coffin-making enterprise is aiming, in part, to provide poor people with an 'equity stake', or a 'trusteeship stake' – as discussed earlier in this chapter. This is a key part of doing economic justice. They are focused on people who are poor and needy, and are working so that these people can participate in God's blessings, including economic blessings.

There is great scope for a range of social institutions to do economic justice in ways such as this. For example, schools can help to equip children and young people from the poorest families with knowledge, understanding and skills ('human capital') that can enable them to earn a living and achieve greater stability – this applies both in the West and in the Majority World.

Community- and church-based groups can do similar things to this. In Ethiopia one of the largest church networks has established many 'self-help groups'.[14] These groups, which meet weekly, were set up with a twofold aim: to enable people, especially women, who are economically poor to learn key skills together, to grow in confidence, and to participate in a 'savings and credit' scheme; and, most importantly, to provide a setting where the good news of Jesus Christ can be shared and discussed. Economic justice – working to give people 'a hand up' out of poverty – and evangelism should go hand in hand.

Many more examples could be given, but there is clearly great scope for doing economic justice in and through a wide range of social – *non*-governmental – institutions and groups.

Subsidiarity – devolving power

As we think about the role of *non*-governmental institutions, it is important to be aware that despite the energy and innovation these often offer, there can still be a desire for 'society' to become the same as 'the state'. That is, there can be a pressure for more and more reliance to be placed on *government* to 'bring economic justice'. This centralizing tendency has been observed by many. One of the most influential organizations in *opposing* this centralizing tendency in socio-economic matters is the Roman Catholic Church. And one of the key elements here is the notion of 'subsidiarity'. This is a central part of what has become known as 'Catholic Social Teaching' (CST). CST has been developed over a number of decades, if not longer.

'Subsidiarity', which is about *helping*, has a close connection with economic justice. One of the clearest statements of what subsidiarity is about comes from a papal document published in 1931:

it is an injustice, a grave evil and a disturbance of right order for a larger and higher organization [such as a national government] to arrogate to itself functions which can be performed efficiently by smaller and lower bodies [such as community groups] . . . Of its nature the true aim of all social activity should be to *help* individual members of the social body, but never to destroy and absorb them.[15]

This notion of subsidiarity seems to fit well with the biblical warnings against centralization on the part of national leaders (and hence governments). And this notion is very important, then, when we think about the role of social (non-governmental) institutions and groups, especially their role in doing economic justice.

Doing economic justice globally

This chapter has already considered some *global* aspects of doing economic justice; for example, we have noted the huge number of people who are still in extreme poverty; we have seen that governments can have a role in keeping in check mega-corporations that have operations across the globe, and have the potential, in a fallen world, to abuse their power through unjust actions; and we have looked at a couple of examples of social (non-governmental) institutions in the Majority World. But in this final section I want to focus briefly on *globalization*. This term refers to the major intensifying of economic *interconnections* (integration) that has been happening across the globe over the past two to three decades. Globalization includes increased trade, the expansion of global capital markets and rapid increases in the pace at which *knowledge* spreads across the world. Is globalization bringing greater economic justice, or greater injustice? How can disciples of Christ, and indeed other people, use any opportunities it offers for doing economic justice – especially with regard to the 10% of the world's population who are in extreme poverty?

Most of us are involved in globalization: we use the worldwide web; many of us have purchased clothes made thousands of miles away; most of us have money in bank and other accounts, and this money is entrusted into the hands of bankers and others who utilize it in electronic financial transactions with the world in a second or two. But is globalization a force for justice or injustice in economic life? I suggest that it is *both, at the same time.*

This stance may seem like sitting on the fence. But there is plenty of evidence that globalization helps to bring *both* beneficial *and* harmful outcomes – not least when assessed according to the biblical norms for economic justice. So it is very important *deliberately* to have this dual assessment regarding globalization. You could call this *deliberate ambivalence* – ambivalence *not* in the sense of 'I am unable to decide,' but in the sense of a deliberate stance, in view of the evidence.

On the positive side, let me repeat what Jim Yong Kim, the World Bank Group President, said in September 2018: 'Over the last 25 years, more than a billion people have lifted themselves out of extreme poverty, and the global poverty rate is now lower than it has ever been in recorded history.'[16]

There is little doubt that the forces of globalization have been a significant contributory factor in this substantial reduction in the number of people in extreme poverty. Higher GDP in a large number of poorer countries, the opportunity to sell across the world products made in the Majority World, the growth in availability of knowledge and finance – all of these aspects of globalization have greatly helped people to lift themselves out of poverty. Essentially, people have been able to *earn a higher income*, through work and employment – and through learning from successes in more developed countries.[17]

Biblical economic justice, as we have seen throughout this book, has a special eye for the poor and needy; and it involves everyone participating in God's blessings, including material blessings. Therefore, it is a positive thing – in terms of economic justice – that many people have been able to lift themselves out of extreme poverty. And globalization has been a significant factor in this.

On the negative side, however, there are two major concerns about globalization. One is that for many people in the Majority World the conditions in which they work are appalling. We saw something of this back in chapter 2. Lots of factories that make items such as trainers have terrible working conditions; many factories even use *forced labour*, modern slavery. The other major concern is that within countries experiencing strong economic growth many people still struggle with extreme poverty. Consider these words from a World Bank Report published in October 2018:

> The most populous countries in South Asia (India and Bangladesh) and Sub-Saharan Africa (Nigeria, Ethiopia, and Democratic Republic of Congo) have the greatest number of extreme poor. India, with over 170 million poor people in 2015, has the highest number of poor people and accounts for nearly a quarter of global poverty.[18]

So the process termed 'globalization' has brought a greater measure of economic justice, yet still permits much injustice. We must hold both aspects together in our minds. There is much debate about other aspects of globalization, and of course there are many complexities. But it is not the purpose of this book to try to assess all of that.[19]

The dual assessment 'deliberate ambivalence' I am giving here is important when it comes to working out what we can *do* to work for economic justice, especially in relation to people in the Majority World. This perspective will help to give an honest approach to considering possible actions and programmes. For example, if there seem to be serious obstacles to tackling extreme poverty in a country or region – as suggested by the World Bank – then it is wise to try to gain some understanding of those obstacles, rather than simply rushing in to some new initiative for trying to deal with poverty.

A major thrust of biblical economic justice is to help give 'a hand up' to people who are economically weak. We have seen that, in practical terms, this means trying to ensure that people can earn a steady income. We have also seen the importance of working to give people an *equity stake*, including skills and knowledge ('human capital'), and a stake in land or capital. How to do that in practice will, of course, involve major challenges – such as issues about who controls land. But that is part of the call to do economic justice.

Conclusion

In this chapter I have tried to provide a way of thinking about doing economic justice in wider society. This book is, as I have said previously, not a 'how to' book. It is vital to have a solid and biblical understanding of the role that national leaders and governments can have in doing economic justice. There is also much that can be done through other social – non-governmental – institutions and groups, as we have seen.

Epilogue

The apostle Peter wrote, 'we are looking forward to a new heaven and a new earth, where righteousness dwells' (2 Peter 3:13). Can you picture this? Can we catch a vision of this?

In the original the word translated here as 'righteousness' is *dikaiosynē*, and as we saw earlier in this book this word also has the sense of *justice*. With all the struggles for justice in this present age and all the complexities can we get a glimpse of this new heaven and earth?

God gave John a revelation of Jesus Christ (Rev. 1:1). Here is part of it:

> Then I saw 'a new heaven and a new earth,' for the first heaven and the first earth had passed away, and there was no longer any sea. I saw the Holy City, the new Jerusalem, coming down out of heaven from God, prepared as a bride beautifully dressed for her husband. And I heard a loud voice from the throne saying, 'Look! God's dwelling-place is now among the people, and he will dwell with them. They will be his people, and God himself will be with them and be their God. "He will wipe every tear from their eyes. There will be no more death" or mourning or crying or pain, for the old order of things has passed away.'
> (Rev. 21:1–4)

As we seek to do economic justice, for God's glory, in this age, let us do so in the light of this glorious future. God's people are pictured as the Holy City, 'the new Jerusalem' – the word means 'city of peace' – transcending whatever 'Jerusalem' has meant in this present age.

It may be hard to believe that this wonderful new heaven and earth will come about – as we live in a highly secularized Western culture with God pushed, seemingly, to the edge of the table, it is easy to lose this vision. But God has *promised* it! And he always keeps his promises, for his word is true and stands for ever. The resurrection of Jesus Christ from the dead is a sure sign of God's power and reality, and of the fact that this Jesus really is the Christ, the Son of the living God. God's sovereignty and actions in his world during the 2,000 years since the resurrection are also powerful evidence to encourage us. Think, for example, of the growth of the church of Christ despite many failings and much persecution. And think of the amazing numbers of people who have become followers of Christ, across the globe, especially over the past 200 years. God's kingdom will not fail.

The vision John saw builds on God's promise through the prophet Isaiah. Can you take time to meditate on this?

See, I will create
   new heavens and a new earth.
The former things will not be remembered,
   nor will they come to mind.
But be glad and rejoice for ever
   in what I will create,
for I will create Jerusalem to be a delight
   and its people a joy.
I will rejoice over Jerusalem
   and take delight in my people;
the sound of weeping and of crying
   will be heard in it no more.
(Isa. 65:17–19)

What a comfort to look forward to this reality in which sorrow and weeping have passed away, once and for all.

As mentioned earlier, the big picture of the Bible is a real-life drama in four acts:

> Creation ⟶ Fall ⟶ Redemption ⟶ New Creation

God's promised work of new creation is what we read about in these glorious passages in Isaiah and Revelation. And the end-time visions in both books include beautiful pictures of justice in economic life. Let us return to Isaiah 65, continuing where we left off above:

> Never again will there be in it
>   an infant who lives but a few days,
>   or an old man who does not live out his years;
> the one who dies at a hundred
>   will be thought a mere child;
> the one who fails to reach a hundred
>   will be considered accursed.
> They will build houses and dwell in them;
>   they will plant vineyards and eat their fruit.
> No longer will they build houses and others live in them,
>   or plant and others eat.
> For as the days of a tree,
>   so will be the days of my people;
> my chosen ones will long enjoy
>   the work of their hands.
> They will not labour in vain,
>   nor will they bear children doomed to misfortune;
> for they will be a people blessed by the LORD,
>   they and their descendants with them.
> (vv. 20–23)

We know it is unjust when others live in a place that is rightfully ours, or eat what is rightfully ours (v. 22). In the new creation that will no longer be the case! Never again! No more injustice in economic life.

We know that this present created order is badly impacted by the fall, by sin and all its consequences – direct and indirect. Verse 23 alludes to two of those impacts: working (labouring) *in vain*, toil with no long-term benefits; and bearing children doomed to misfortune. But God gives Isaiah a glimpse of his new creation where all such negative consequences will be in the past, never to occur again. The fruits of work will be long enjoyed (v. 22). There will be no more misfortune, no more weeping. Justice and joy will dominate economic life and relationships. And all to the glory of God.

As far as I can see, the Bible gives little detail about what life will be like, day to day, in the new creation. But it is a new creation! It will have some kind of material dimension: the resurrection body of Jesus Christ – a physical body – bears powerful witness to this, and assures us of this. The Garden of Eden in Genesis 1 – 2 becomes the Garden City in Revelation 21 – 22. There will surely be a material and economic dimension in this new creation. But no more injustice or weeping.

Justice and judgment, repentance and faith

Jesus Christ 'will come again with glory to judge both the living and the dead'. These words from one of the historic confessions of Christian faith, the Nicene Creed, are a crucial reminder of the decisions you and I must make. At the end of this age – when Christ comes again – there will be a final judgment. The new creation will be the home of righteousness, the home of justice. But will you be part of it, or not? The invitation of Jesus Christ is available to everyone, without distinction (Mark 1:14–15): 'Jesus went into Galilee, proclaiming the good news of God. "The time has come," he said. "The kingdom of God has come near. Repent and believe the good news!"'

The kingdom of God is indeed good news: the good news of God's saving rule with Christ as king. But how does anyone enter this kingdom? By repentance and faith. To repent means to acknowledge our sin – wrongdoing and rebellion – against God, and to turn back to him. To believe the good news is to trust in Jesus Christ and his death on the cross in our place, taking the punishment that we as sinners deserve.

This is the crucial decision that each of us faces. Will we turn back to God in repentance and faith or not?

Listen to the words of the apostle Peter, spoken in the Mediterranean seaport of Caesarea, as he tells his hearers what he and his colleagues know concerning Jesus Christ of Nazareth:

> We are witnesses of everything he did in the country of the Jews and in Jerusalem. They killed him by hanging him on a cross, but God raised him from the dead on the third day and caused him to be seen. He was not seen by all the people, but by witnesses whom God had already chosen – by us who ate and drank with him after he rose from the dead. He commanded us to preach to the people and to testify that he is the one whom God appointed as judge of the living and the dead. All the prophets testify about him that everyone who believes in him receives forgiveness of sins through his name.
> (Acts 10:39–43)

God is just and merciful. He offers us a way of being saved from the just judgment we deserve. I would urge you to pause and take stock, and if you have not already come to know and trust this God through his Son Jesus Christ, then to make it a priority to enquire much further into these things.

As this book comes to a close let me share a wonderful passage from the Old Testament about this Christ and the justice he brings and will bring. Centuries before the first coming of Jesus Christ to earth, the Jesus who lived at Nazareth in Galilee, the prophet Isaiah foretold his coming, as God by his Spirit moved him. A term Isaiah gives for the one who was to come is the *servant* of the Lord. Of him God says:

> Here is my servant, whom I uphold,
>   my chosen one in whom I delight;
> I will put my Spirit on him,
>   and he will bring justice to the nations.

He will not shout or cry out,
    or raise his voice in the streets.
A bruised reed he will not break,
    and a smouldering wick he will not snuff out.
In faithfulness he will bring forth justice;
    he will not falter or be discouraged
till he establishes justice on earth.
    In his teaching the islands will put their hope.
(Isa. 42:1–4)

To speak of 'the islands' is a way of referring to people living in even the most distant places – the remotest islands. Wherever people are, anywhere on earth, near or far, they can put their hope in this Jesus Christ, who in his grace came all the way from heaven down to this earth, who came to save and establish justice.

Points for reflection, discussion and action

1 What *is* economic justice?

1 This chapter has argued that, in today's world, there is great confusion about what 'economic justice' is. If you had not read this chapter, would you have said that 'justice' is based on *rights*, *needs* or *merit* (*desert*)?

2 If justice is rooted in *who God is* – his character and nature – how significant is that? What difference does that make?

3 This chapter argues that God has built justice into creation. The world God has created, and sustains, includes a *just order*. How is this different from a purely secular or non-Christian way of viewing the world?

4 This chapter sets out four key aspects of a biblical understanding of economic justice. Which of these surprises you most? How different is *this* understanding of economic justice from how other people in the twenty-first century think of 'economic justice'?

5 Economic justice means treating people in line with God's principles for how we are to live in the economic dimensions of life. God has given his norms and principles in order for us as human beings to flourish. Do you view God's commands in the Bible simply as 'rules to be obeyed'? Or as norms to help us flourish? Or both?

6 To know this God – to be in relationship with him – *means* defending the cause of the poor and needy. How persuaded are you that concern for the poor is part of what it means to do economic justice? What might this mean in practice for you?

7 This chapter argues that economic justice includes *relationships* and reciprocal responsibilities. Does this surprise you? What do you make of the biblical examples of this as presented in the chapter?

8 The fourth aspect of biblical economic justice according to the chapter is, 'Justice in the allocation of resources means that everyone participates in God's blessings, including material blessings.' How different is *this* understanding from the idea of justice as numerical 'equality'? Are you comfortable or un-comfortable with this biblical emphasis? What do you think are some of the practical implications of this?

2 Doing justice as consumers

1 This chapter reports that '71% of fashion companies indicate there is probably slavery in their supply chains'. What is your response to this information?

2 The chapter suggests that we could do some quick Internet research regarding a firm that may be involved in sub-stantial *underpayments* to staff, somewhere along the supply chain; or regarding companies that are widely seen to be failing in their moral responsibility for just treatment of em-ployees, and for monitoring their own supply chains in that regard. What do you make of these suggestions? How could you follow them up? How else might you act with justice *as a consumer*?

3 This chapter offers a critique of 'ethical shopping'. How do you respond to this critique?

4 'We face, then, a clear choice between, on the one hand, consumerism and a love of money, or, on the other hand, love for God and a seeking of his justice. That is why subverting consumerism is fundamental to doing economic justice.' This deep-level choice must be made. What do you make of this?

5 What is your own attitude towards the money God has entrusted to you? What place does the love of money have in your heart? If you think that some change is required of you, how will you go about trying to change?

6 The chapter has made suggestions about how justice can influence *what* we buy; for example, in the use of 'discretionary money' that we may have. How could all this make a difference to the way you engage with the world around you?

7 'To do economic justice, as consumers, involves treating rightly every person with whom we come into contact. This is a mindset that is totally opposed to that of the prevailing consumerist culture. So there is a full-on clash here.' Do you recognize this clash? What might you do about it?

3 Doing justice in the workplace

1 'A job is just a way of earning money.' In 2015 49% of people surveyed in the UK said that they *agreed* with that statement. What about you? Do you agree with it, or not? Why?

2 The chapter argues that 'work – purposeful and productive activity as stewards of creation – has a central place in God's big picture', his big picture of redemption. Do you ever think of your work in these terms? In what ways might your work be a setting where God can be bringing restoration from the effects of sin and the fall?

3 The chapter argues that the Bible gives *radical* teaching about doing justice in the workplace? To what extent do you agree that this teaching, especially in Colossians and Ephesians, is radical?

4 This chapter talks a lot about 'our relationships in the workplace'. Have you ever thought about 'economic justice' in terms of your workplace relationships? How will you let the biblical teaching on all of this impact you in day-to-day practice?

5 The chapter gives four areas where *managers* can do economic justice in their relationships. What do you make of these suggestions? If you have management responsibilities, how could you put these suggestions into practice?

6 'For many people, work is about meeting *my* needs, attaining *my* goals, fulfilling *my* career plan and earning money for *my* leisure time.' To what extent does this resonate with your experience? In working situations of which you are aware – directly or indirectly – what are the key aspects of the workplace

mindset? How as Christians can we be a counterculture for Christ, in the workplace?

7 How can we pray more effectively for one another about doing economic justice in the workplace?

4 Church communities: beacons of economic justice

1 Think about the church community of which you are a part (if you are a follower of Jesus Christ). Is being *a beacon of justice* part of that church's vision? If not, why do you think that is the case?

2 This chapter sets out two interrelated biblical principles for local church communities: compassionate provision for the poor and needy, and enabling the poor and needy, wherever possible, to earn a living. What do you make of these two intertwined principles? Does anything about them surprise you?

3 This chapter – and the book overall – argues that we can derive *principles* from the material in the Old Testament and New Testament, and that these must be applied to our behaviour today, as Christians and church communities. Are you familiar with this kind of method of studying the Bible and putting it into practice? Can you think of other biblical material from which we can derive moral and socio-economic principles in this kind of way?

4 What dangers might there be in attempting to use this kind of approach? How can we guard against those dangers?

5 'There should be no poor . . . there will always be poor people . . .' This chapter highlighted the tension between those two phrases, as recorded in the Bible. In what ways do you think that same tension is relevant in your local church context?

6 How does *your* church organize and administer provision for the poor within the church family? If you do not know, how can you find out? What more should your church be doing, in the light of this chapter?

7 What can your church community do to help poorer church members, wherever possible, get to the point where they can support themselves and their household?

8 If your church community is based in a more affluent area, and does not seem to have many poorer people within it, how can you apply the biblical call to have a special eye for the poor and needy? What might a partnership with a church from a less well-off area look like?

9 How can your church support the poor and needy *outside* your community? Consider the practical examples of this, as mentioned in this chapter. How might you adopt some of those ideas in your context? Are you and your church community involved in any way with credit unions, or other initiatives to help the poor and needy in matters of finance? (E.g. Christians Against Poverty money advice courses.) If not, how could this chapter get you started in thinking and action in such ways?

10 The final section of this chapter is headed 'doing justice and preaching grace', and argues strongly that these belong together. How is your church community doing here? Is it stronger on one or the other of these two? How can they be held together in practice in your setting?

5 Firms and corporations

1 This chapter focuses on how disciples of Christ can influence – for greater economic justice – the organizations in which they work, and help to lead or manage. This emphasis is different from that in chapter 3, which emphasized personal relationships in the workplace. What do you think about this idea of influencing the organizations in which we may work? How desirable is this, from a biblical perspective? How feasible is this?

2 The chapter argues that economic justice, biblically, is not simply a *situation*: it is about how people are treated, both by other people and by human institutions. To what extent are you persuaded about this? How does this approach differ from other ideas about what 'economic justice' is?

3 Think about some of the real-world contexts that you know about – companies and corporations. This could include a company for which you work or in which you have a management

role. How do any of these companies seem to be doing with regard to God's norms for economic justice? (The chapter gives more criteria and questions you could use here.)

4 The chapter argues that making a profit and doing economic justice can easily go hand in hand. Do you agree? When might they *not* go hand in hand?

5 'By helping to provide paid work, firms can help do economic justice.' How do you respond to this?

6 How can powerful corporations do more to treat properly those employees with low wages who are in a weaker position?

7 What can large companies do to act more justly, when they face the constraints of shareholders who demand a high rate of return on their investment?

8 The chapter argues that recent trends in corporate executive pay raise serious questions regarding economic justice. What do you make of this? What can Christians in positions of senior responsibility do to balance the key factors here?

6 Banks and other financial institutions

1 What is your attitude towards the money God has entrusted to you? What place does the love of money have in your heart?

2 'Greed . . . is idolatry,' says the New Testament (Col. 3:5). Yet greed is a powerful motivator in Western societies today. To what extent is such greed present in your mindset? How can you gain the spiritual resources to overcome such greed?

3 This chapter has argued that excessive lending and borrowing involve injustice, as well as being unwise. How much (if anything) do you owe at present? (That includes mortgages, credit card debt, car finance loans and bank overdrafts.) How, in the light of the biblical teaching we have discussed, should you view borrowing? If you do owe some money (either to an individual or to a financial institution), have you ever considered that you have a *relationship* with the lender? What difference should that make to your attitude as a borrower?

4 Consider what this chapter has emphasized as key aspects of biblical economic justice. If you work for a bank or other

financial institution, what do you think are the most important challenges and questions raised in this chapter for your organization? Where do you think your organization might be acting unjustly? If you are a follower of Jesus Christ, what could you and other Christians do to influence your bank (employer) to behave in a manner more consistent with the biblical norms of justice? If you are in a managerial position, what are the opportunities for change in a more just direction? How can you influence the dominant values in the organization?

5 If you work for a bank or financial institution, how can you do economic justice more fully in your own behaviour *day to day*? (You may have different options here, depending on your position in the organization.) Whatever your position, what would it mean for you in your relationships at work to act for what is just?

6 Many, if not all, of us have accounts with a bank or other financial institution. Have you ever considered switching to a different bank on the grounds of unjust behaviour by your bank? How can the biblical teaching presented in this chapter be applied to the question of where you put your savings?

7 This chapter has argued that on biblical grounds any loans to the poor and needy should be made *only* on a compassionate, and not a profit-making, basis. To what extent do you agree? If you are linked in any way to a 'payday' lender, or similar, how will this chapter affect your thinking and behaviour?

8 What scope can you see for people – whether banks, socially driven enterprises or others – to set up, and/or invest in, alternative and *low*-cost compassionate loans for those who are poor or on low incomes? In what ways might you or others you know be able to play a part in this?

9 The financial crisis that began in 2007 has had a huge and damaging impact. This chapter has argued that greed, pride, folly and hubris played a significant part in this crisis. Does that sound plausible to you? Take some time to reflect on the state of the culture of which you are a part. Where can you see greed and pride at work? How does the Christian gospel of repentance

and faith in Jesus Christ speak into this culture? How can you use this as a starting point for talking to non-Christians about the gospel?

7 Wider society: nationally and globally

1 Is there too much inequality of income and wealth? How much of a role should the state play in economic and social life? The chapter argues that questions such as these are controversial, especially across the left–right political spectrum. Where, if anywhere, would you position yourself on that spectrum? And why?

2 The chapter presents some data and trends regarding global absolute poverty, income and inequality. Does anything surprise you about these statistics?

3 This chapter argues that 'the Bible does not delegate economic justice to the government – instead, everyone has responsibility for doing economic justice'. Do you agree or disagree? Why?

4 'The principles of biblical economic justice can be applied all the way across the left–right political spectrum; that is, in countries that have a greater role for the government in economic life, and in those that have a lesser role for it.' To what extent do you agree?

5 The chapter argues that in the biblical vision of economic justice, 'What matters is not some numerical measure of equality, but that each individual and household has a meaningful stake and is flourishing.' In what ways do you think that such an *equity* or *trusteeship stake* could make a difference in your context?

6 This chapter argues that there is a role – in economic justice – for those in authority to uphold laws that reflect the ethical teachings of the Bible, to focus on those who are economically weak and to step in and act where there is economic oppression. What do you make of this? Thinking about your context, in which of these three areas do you think those in authority should be doing more? Any suggestions for how to help bring this about?

7 There is 'great scope for doing economic justice in and through a wide range of social – *non*-governmental – institutions and groups'. The chapter gives some current examples. What ideas and suggestions can you be exploring? Try to consider both the national and global context.

8 The book began – back in the introduction – with a call for Christians to engage confidently with the world around us, for the sake of the gospel. Doing economic justice is part of this confident engagement. 'It is by living and working in the world – including in the economic dimension – that we will have greater opportunity to testify to people about the good news of Jesus Christ.' In what ways can you see these greater opportunities being possible in your context?

9 God has promised to bring about a 'new heaven and new earth' – the home of righteousness and justice. The final chapter of the book talks about this. What difference does it make to have this eternal or new creation perspective? How should this have an impact now on your thinking, praying and actions?

Notes

Introduction

1 See <www.licc.org.uk/about-licc>, accessed 27 March 2015.

2 Os Guinness, *Renaissance: The Power of the Gospel However Dark the Times* (Downers Grove: InterVarsity Press, 2014), p. 28 (emphasis original).

3 Ibid., p. 88.

1 What *is* economic justice?

1 See <www.webster-dictionary.org/definition/justice>, accessed 14 June 2018.

2 In much of the literature on justice these two categories are termed, respectively, 'commutative justice' and 'distributive justice'. For a detailed discussion, see my previous book *What Is Economic Justice? Biblical and Secular Perspectives Contrasted* (Carlisle: Paternoster, 2007), ch. 5.

3 The underlying explanation for this feature may well be to do with the fact there is no prevailing view about what the *foundation* for justice is – a point already discussed in this chapter. To combine an understanding of both justice in production and exchange *and* justice in distribution may be impossible unless there is a deeper foundation for justice.

4 Like many verses in the OT, this verse links very closely two vital words, 'righteous' and 'justice'. In a huge number of places in the OT 'righteousness' and 'justice' come as a pair; e.g. Pss 37:6; 48:10–11; Jer. 22:3. More will be said about this in later pages of this book. For a fuller discussion, see my *What Is Economic Justice?*, ch. 2.

5 For a few examples, see Pss 19:7–14; 119 as a whole; Exod. 20; Heb. 1:1–2; 2 Tim. 3:14–17; John 17:17; and Mark 7:1–13 (ESVUK), where Jesus Christ – in the midst of a dialogue/debate with the Pharisees –

says almost in passing that the Scriptures are 'the commandment of God' (v. 8) and 'the word of God' (v. 13).

6 Throughout this chapter (and this book as a whole) I refer to 'a biblical understanding of economic justice', not '*the* biblical understanding'. This use of the indefinite (rather than the definite) article is deliberate. Although I am confident that the Bible gives us the truth about what economic justice is, I am less confident about my own ability (especially as an imperfect human being – a sinner like all my readers!) both to comprehend fully what the Bible teaches, and to put the biblical material into words. So, even though I have sought for years to share with others my attempts to deepen and strengthen my grasp of the biblical material about economic justice, and to learn alongside them within the community of Christian faith, many flaws doubtless remain in my grasp and presentation of all this. Hence what is offered here is only '*a*' biblical understanding of economic justice.

In my previous book I have written much more extensively about the biblical basis for the understanding of economic justice that I am putting forward in this book. See my *What Is Economic Justice?* That book in turn was based on my 2003 PhD thesis (King's College, London).

7 In chapter 2 of this book I discuss in more detail the Bible's main words for 'righteousness' and 'justice'.

8 There is similar instruction in Lev. 19:35–36.

9 Paul teaches the same principle in 1 Cor. 9:1–14, and again includes the teaching of the Lord Jesus as part of his reasoning (v. 14).

10 Much biblical material presents this kind of emphasis; see e.g. Deut. 7:6–11.

11 Again the Bible contains much material that emphasizes this; see e.g. the whole of Deut. 6.

12 'Justice' in v. 14 translates *mišpāṭ* in the original language. Similarly, in the next verse that I quote in the main text, Ps. 103:6.

13 Here 'justice' translates the Hebrew word *dîn*, and 'cause' translates *mišpāṭ*.

14 Note that in v. 13 it is a matter of *injustice* that workers are not being paid. By implication, it is a matter of *doing justice* that workers are

paid properly. This is a further example of what I argued in the previous few pages, namely that economic justice is, fundamentally, about treating people appropriately, according to the norms and principles given by God.

15 In v. 15 'just' translates the Hebrew word *mišpāṭ*.

16 In v. 4 'justice' translates the word *mîšôr* from the Hebrew original. The RSV translates it as 'equity'.

17 In v. 17 'justice' translates *mišpāṭ* in the Hebrew.

18 Deut. 10:17–19 makes a similar and powerful link from God's loving treatment of people – including the resident foreigner – to how Israel should love the foreigner.

19 For more details, using similar categories, see Michael Schluter, 'Christian Morality Relating to Credit and Debt', in Andrew Hartropp (ed.), *Families in Debt: The Nature, Causes and Effects of Debt Problems and Policy Proposals for Their Alleviation*, Jubilee Centre Research Paper 7 (Cambridge: Jubilee Centre, 1988), pp. 3–17.

20 A related requirement – spelt out in the following verses in Deut. 15 – was that a fellow Israelite who had been sold (as a kind of 'bonded servant') to someone else had, in the seventh year, to be set free. (Such cases would normally arise only in the context of extreme poverty and destitution; see Lev. 25:35–46.)

21 Please note that this was a point of detail in the teachings given for this society at this time. Taking the Bible as a whole, I do not think that this socio-economic arrangement is presented as a timeless principle to be applied to all societies. In later chapters I discuss in more depth the issue of how to apply specific biblical teachings to different contexts.

22 See John D. Mason, 'Assistance Programmes in the Bible', *Transformation* 4.2 (April–June 1987), pp. 1–14.

23 People sometimes question whether or not any such 'Jubilee' ever happened. For now, my response is, 'That is beside the point!' The point here revolves around the norms and principles given by God. If the people of God failed to act according to these principles, then such inaction in no way undermines the principles themselves.

2 Doing justice as consumers

1 See 'Unboxing the Truth', <www.trust.org/unboxing-the-truth>, accessed 20 July 2018.

2 Since the UK referendum vote in 2016 in favour of the UK's leaving the European Union (EU), discussions about supply chains have formed a central part of the debates concerning Brexit. This is because of the strong economic and industrial interconnections between the UK and the rest of the EU. As at the time of completing this book (spring 2019), the details of what form Brexit would take – and indeed the question of whether or not the UK would in reality leave the EU – still remained unresolved.

3 See '5 Supply Chain Management Tips', <www.raconteur.net/ business/5-supply-chain-management-tips>, accessed 20 July 2018.

4 At the time of writing there is some discussion about whether supply chains may become *slightly* simpler in the future – but only slightly so.

5 A quick Internet search for, say, 'supply chain injustice' will point you to a huge number of resources dedicated to helping companies deal with the moral challenges of supply chains.

6 See 'Unboxing the Truth'.

7 A possible argument against my suggestion here – about perhaps shopping elsewhere – is that by *not* spending money on the products of the company prone to injustice, then we would harm further the exploited workers: because they might even lose their jobs if the company lost sales and had to shut down. This is not really a solid counterargument. If I want to help exploited workers (from a vast distance especially), probably the most effective way to do so is to play my part in supporting the better and more just companies, by buying their products. In time, very possibly, 'the good money will drive out the bad'; i.e. companies that operate according to good moral values and are well run are more likely to survive and grow than those that do not. The other thing I could do is specifically to join a campaign designed to force the unjust company to behave better. But simply to carry on 'feeding the unjust company' (continuing to buy their products) is, by itself, not likely to bring any change for the better.

8 E.g. the 'Ethical Consumer' website <www.ethicalconsumer.org>, accessed 7 August 2018, includes both of these features.

9 I explain this in detail in my book *What Is Economic Justice? Biblical and Secular Perspectives Contrasted* (Carlisle: Paternoster, 2007), ch. 2, esp. pp. 15–17.

10 In the Greek the word family includes *dikaios* (just, right) and *dikaiosynē* (justice, righteousness). See e.g. Rom. 1:17; 3:21–26; 4:1–6, 9–12; Gal. 2:15–21; 3:6–14.

11 It is also the case that suppliers seek to influence the thoughts, emotions and behaviour of consumers – sometimes deliberately. (Think of all the money spent by companies on marketing and advertising.) But that does not detract from the point that consumers themselves often have considerable influence.

12 One might conceivably term these items 'necessities', but I am wary of using the language of 'necessities' and 'needs' – and of using the term 'luxuries' for spending on 'non-necessities'. My wariness is because this kind of language makes it sound as though it is a fact as to which things are 'needs' and which are 'luxuries'; but in reality there is quite a lot of *subjective* evaluation – one person's 'luxury' can often seem to be another person's 'need'.

13 This definition comes from <www.startups.co.uk/what-is-social-enterprise>, accessed 14 August 2018.

14 The option of *lending* money to people who are in need – a principle clearly set out in the OT, as we saw in the previous chapter – will be explored further in a later chapter, in the context of our doing economic justice *as local church gatherings*.

3 Doing justice in the workplace

1 See <www.leadersinheels.com/career/6-management-styles-and-when-best-to-use-them-the-leaders-tool-kit>, accessed 21 August 2018.

2 *British Social Attitudes 33*, 2016 edition (published July). Available at <www.bsa.natcen.ac.uk/latest-report/british-social-attitudes-33/work.aspx>, accessed 20 August 2018.

3 Many scholars have written about this. See e.g. Donald Hay, *Economics Today: A Christian Critique* (Leicester: Apollos, 1989),

pp. 73–75; Alan Storkey, *Transforming Economics: A Christian Way to Employment* (London: SPCK, 1986), ch. 5.

4 Michael Rhodes and Robby Holt with Brian Fikkert, *Practicing the King's Economy: Honoring Jesus in How We Work, Earn, Spend, Save and Give* (Grand Rapids: Baker, 2018), p. 40.

5 Ibid., citing Campbell R. McConnell and Stanley L. Brue, *Economics: Principles, Problems and Policies*, 13th edn (New York: McGraw-Hill, 1996), p. 1.

6 Col. 1:15–20 gives a wonderful and more expansive description of God's new-creation promise in Christ.

7 The parallel passage is Col. 3:1–10.

8 The parallel passage is Eph. 6:5–9.

9 In the Greek 'justly' is again a translation of the word *dikaios*. A more literal translation of the original would be, 'grant what is just [*dikaios*] and fair to your bondservants'.

10 See Peter T. O'Brien, *Colossians, Philemon*, WBC (Word: Waco, 1982), p. 232.

11 For more details, see Bible commentaries such as ibid.

12 See e.g. the article 'Slave', in the *Illustrated Bible Dictionary*, ed. J. D. Douglas et al. (Leicester: Inter-Varsity Press, 1980), part 3, pp. 1464–1466.

13 Paul's letter to Philemon is also widely recognized as serving to undermine the institution of slavery: Philemon has a slave named Onesimus, who ran away; both are now believers in Jesus Christ. Paul says to Philemon (vv. 15–16), 'Perhaps the reason he [Onesimus] was separated from you for a little while was that you might have him back for ever – no longer as a slave, but better than a slave, as a dear brother. He is very dear to me but even dearer to you, both as a fellow man and as a brother in the Lord.' New relationships in Christ mean that Onesimus is no longer to be seen as a 'slave'.

14 In the Greek the word for 'masters' is the same word as that for 'Lord' (v. 22), *kyrios*.

15 Again the word for 'master' is *kyrios*, often translated as 'Lord'.

16 See <www.clarabridge.com/blog/employees-your-most-important-asset>, accessed 28 August 2018.

17 Rodger Dean Duncan, <www.forbes.com/sites/forbesleadershipforum/ 2013/08/20/nine-ways-to-keep-your-companys-most-valuable-asset-its-employees/#766579e32eab>, accessed 28 August 2018; emphasis original.

18 Ibid.

19 Ibid.

4 Church communities: beacons of economic justice

1 Acts 9 reports that Tabitha became sick and died, but, wonderfully, God used the apostle Peter to raise her back to life! Go to Acts 9 for the full story.

2 The other key aspects of economic justice – e.g. treating people appropriately in *economic* relationships – do not apply with such relevance to church communities: relationships *within* church communities do not often involve buying and selling to one another. When e.g. coffee is served after church gatherings, it is often provided free. And if there is a bowl for voluntary donations, they really are (I hope) voluntary. Some church communities do employ a minister and perhaps other workers, and so there are questions here of fair payment; but chapter 2 (above) has already talked about the important biblical principle that a labourer is worthy of his hire – which was applied in the NT in a *church* context. So there is little to add here.

3 The OT material is superbly explained by Chris Wright; see e.g. Chris Wright, *Old Testament Ethics for the People of God* (Leicester: Inter-Varsity Press, 2004). Wright often uses the term 'paradigm' in relation to the package or framework of teaching, laws and provisions given in the OT, in order to convey both the importance of appreciating the whole package (i.e. we are *not* to 'pick and choose' isolated bits as we wish), and the sense that this framework/ package has relevance for the people of God *today*. Clearly, the question of *how* we are faithfully to apply the OT today is very important: the present book seeks to give plenty of guidelines for how we can do that.

4 I am not here trying to present a comprehensive overview of the OT material – see the work of Chris Wright (previous note) for an excellent analysis of that – or the NT material.

5 Most if not all people in the West today, whether Christian believers or not, would accept this principle: we can give thanks for this; the fact that people do accept this may well have something to do, in turn, with the enormous influence Judaeo-Christian thinking has had in the West over many centuries. So it is helpful as well as important to delve into the foundations of this Judaeo-Christian thinking: the OT and NT.

6 As noted in chapter 2 above, it seems likely that the 'third year' was specific to a given field; i.e. in any calendar year at least some fields would be in their 'third year'. This in turn would mean that in *every* calendar year food was coming in for these (potentially) vulnerable groups.

7 This requirement is stated also in Lev. 19:9–10 and Deut. 24:19–22. For a comprehensive and very helpful analysis of the OT teachings and practices, see Roland de Vaux, *Ancient Israel: Its Life and Institutions* (London: DLT, 1973).

8 For a recent and very helpful explanation of Lev. 25, see Michael Rhodes and Robby Holt with Brian Fikkert, *Practicing the King's Economy: Honoring Jesus in How We Work, Earn, Spend, Save and Give* (Grand Rapids: Baker, 2018), ch. 7.

9 V. 28 of Lev. 25 goes on to require that in the Jubilee year the land, in the event that it was not redeemed in the meantime, would be returned to the original owner.

10 Professor Muhammad Yunus won the Nobel Prize for his pioneering work in this field. 'Recipient of the 2006 Nobel Peace Prize, Professor Muhammad Yunus is internationally recognized for his work in poverty alleviation and the empowerment of poor women. Professor Yunus has successfully melded capitalism with social responsibility to create the Grameen Bank, a microcredit institution committed to providing small amounts of working capital to the poor for self-employment. From its origins as an action-research project in 1976, Grameen Bank has grown to provide collateral-free loans to 7.5 million clients in more than 82,072 villages in Bangladesh and 97% of whom are women.' See <www.grameenfoundation.org/muhammad-yunus>, accessed 10 October 2018. Microcredit (or microfinance) is now offered

by a wide range of institutions, many of them established on a Christian foundation.

11 There has been much debate about the idea of loans at zero interest and/or low interest, including questions about whether or not interest of any amount is ever valid, morally; and if it is, then under what conditions. But in this book I am not going to engage with these debates in any depth. Essentially, my approach is to argue that the OT presents (among other things) a *principle* (or norm) regarding the importance of compassionate loans to the poor that are designed to be a 'hand up', and are *not* given primarily for commercial gain. This principle has clear biblical support, I argue, and is of great relevance for today's world. For a discussion of some of the issues around interest, with contrasting views, see e.g. Paul Mills, 'Finance', in Michael Schluter and John Ashcroft (eds.), *Jubilee Manifesto: A Framework, Agenda and Strategy for Christian Social Reform* (Leicester: Inter-Varsity Press, 2005), pp. 196–215; Ben Cooper, *The Ethics of Usury*, Latimer Studies 77 (London: Latimer Trust, 2012).

12 Some other English translations have 'will' rather than 'should', and this emphasizes the *promise* aspect here; but this promise (purpose) is still linked closely with *obedience* on the part of the people of Israel. If the promise (purpose) was not fulfilled, that lack was down to the disobedience of the people.

13 The tension here is somewhat similar to the tension regarding the kingdom of God: it has dawned, and in that sense 'has come'; and yet it will not come in full until after Jesus Christ returns in glory to judge the living and the dead. Has the kingdom of God come yet? Yes and no!

14 See also the related accounts in Mark 14:1–11 and Matt. 26:6–13. In these verses Jesus states that 'the poor you will always have with you' (Mark 14:7) – reflecting *one* of the emphases in Deut. 15 (as we have already seen) – and they are able to help the poor at any time they are willing to do so (which should of course be at all times); *but* 'you will not always have me', he goes on to say (Mark 14:7). The woman who anointed him had done a beautiful thing, Christ says. The contrast is between 'always' and 'not always'. Christ is clearly *not* saying that help for the poor is optional: quite the opposite.

15 The text of Acts 4:34–35 makes it clear that – despite suggestions in more recent times – what the early church practised was not some kind of 'total communism', with *all* property sold and *no one* retaining possession; rather, it was 'from time to time'. In the Greek the verb 'sold' is in the imperfect tense, which suggests that people were not selling everything at once. Hence the NIV's translation 'from time to time'. They were certainly in the habit of selling their property, however, in order to ensure that everyone's needs were met. In the case of Ananias and Sapphira, reported in the verses that follow (Acts 5:1–11), their sin was that some property was sold *but* Ananias – with his wife Sapphira's full knowledge – kept some of the proceeds for himself; in so doing, he did not lie to people 'but to God' (5:4).

16 Paul reports his intentions regarding this collection in his letter to the believers in Rome (Rom. 15:25–31), and mentions the results in the context of his trial before the Roman governor Felix (Acts 24:17). In 2 Cor. 8 – 9 Paul urges the Christians at Corinth to follow the generous example of the believers in Macedonia by adding to the sacrificial contributions made by the Macedonians to this collection, thanks to God's grace (e.g. 2 Cor. 8:1, 10–11).

17 Acts 6:1 reports that Grecian Jews complained against Hebraic Jews because the former's widows were being overlooked in the daily food distribution. The outcome was the creation of the category of 'deacons' to be in charge of the food ministry, in order to release the apostles to focus on prayer and the ministry of the word of God (v. 4).

18 Bruce W. Winter, *Seek the Welfare of the City: Christians as Benefactors and Citizens* (Grand Rapids: Eerdmans; Carlisle: Paternoster, 1994), p. 64.

19 Rhodes, Holt and Fikkert, *Practicing the King's Economy*, p. 142.

20 As with other chapters in this book, I am not seeking to provide any kind of 'detailed manual'. That would be beyond the scope here, and well beyond my abilities!

21 If at some point individuals or households make it plain that they are content with the wider church community knowing about their plight and their take-up of the church's provision, then that is fine – but it should be the former's decision.

22 The Trussell Trust has done much on the former, and Christians Against Poverty on the latter.

23 Rhodes, Holt and Fikkert, *Practicing the King's Economy*, p. 115. Evidently, there is funding behind the scenes for this whole operation.

24 Ibid., p. 115.

25 Tim Chester and Steve Timmis very helpfully bring out this emphasis on relationships, for both word and deed ministry, in their book *Total Church: A Radical Reshaping Around Gospel and Community* (Nottingham: Inter-Varsity Press, 2007).

26 See Christopher J. H. Wright, *The Mission of God: Unlocking the Bible's Grand Narrative* (Nottingham: Inter-Varsity Press, 2006).

27 See e.g. Kevin DeYoung and Greg Gilbert, *What Is the Mission of the Church? Making Sense of Social Justice, Shalom and the Great Commission* (Wheaton: Crossway, 2011).

28 See Andrew Hartropp and Oddvar Sten Ronsen, 'Evangelism Lost? A Need to Redefine Christian Integral Mission', *Mission Studies* 33.1 (2016), pp. 66–84.

5 Firms and corporations

1 The role of non-profit organizations (including social enterprises) would also merit attention here, but space prevents a detailed treatment. Recent years have seen a growing number of 'social enterprises', a term that covers a broad spectrum of organizations, but all seeking to combine (in various ways) social goals with entrepreneurial and business-type initiative and rigour.

2 See <www.ippr.org/research/publications/prosperity-and-justice>, accessed 30 October 2018. The CEJ offers six principles of economic justice (pp. 24–25); these share some common ground with the biblically rooted understanding of economic justice put forward in this book. However, there are also some crucial differences; e.g. the CEJ does *not* say that doing economic justice includes an emphasis on the quality of relationships; and it does not seem to have an understanding of reciprocal obligations in economic relationships. Not surprisingly the CEJ is not seeking to build on biblical foundations; and thus it is not in a position to acknowledge the

importance of God's principles for doing economic justice,
as revealed in the Bible.

3 CEJ report, 'Executive Summary', p. 4. The executive summary is
available at <www.ippr.org/research/publications/prosperity-and-
justice-executive-summary>, accessed 30 October 2018.

4 Milton Friedman, *Capitalism and Freedom*, 40th edn (Chicago:
University of Chicago Press, 2002), p. 133; emphasis added; cited
on the Becker Friedman Institute (University of Chicago) website,
<www.bfi.uchicago.edu/news/feature-story/corporate-social-
responsibilty-friedmans-view>, accessed 30 October 2018. Part
of what Friedman was arguing was that a firm should focus on
what it is best at doing – being as efficient as possible (for which
increased profits provide a good barometer) – rather than directly
trying to work out what is 'best for society'. But the (indirect)
outworking of being efficient would be that society ends up being
better off; e.g. because resources are allocated more efficiently than
otherwise, and so everyone has more goods and services to enjoy
than would otherwise be the case. Hence Friedman's language of
the 'social responsibility of business'. I would argue that firms do
have a *moral responsibility* to act justly as they go about seeking
to be efficient; i.e. that doing justice and making profit need to be
integrated.

5 'Other things being equal' is a favourite term of economists when
doing this kind of analysis. In practice, however, 'other things' are
often *not* equal! For example, a cut in wages to some employees may
provoke a negative reaction from *other* employees; and/or a negative
reaction from consumers/customers who learn of the firm's wage cut
to the weakest; and so on.

6 This is a complex area. For a useful overview (with application
to the USA context), see Duane Windsor, 'Shareholder Wealth
Maximization', in John R. Boatright, *Finance Ethics: Critical Issues
in Theory and Practice* (New Jersey: Wiley, 2010), ch. 23.

7 By including the 'environment' in a list where the other items
comprise *people*, we are in a sense personalizing the environment;
but this is only a linguistic device or convenience – I am *not*
attributing personal being to the physical environment!

8 For a helpful and detailed review of the legal position in the UK –
in the light of the 2006 Companies Act – see John Davies, 'A Guide
to Directors' Responsibilities Under the Companies Act 2006'
(published by the Association of Chartered Certified Accountants),
<www.accaglobal.com/content/dam/acca/global/PDF-technical/
business-law/tech-tp-cdd.pdf>, accessed 31 October 2018.

9 There are some detailed and technical questions about the
relationship between *short-run* and *long-run* profit-maximization,
in relation to SVM, but these need not detain us here.

10 See e.g. <www.gov.uk/government/consultations/corporate-
responsibility-call-for-views>, accessed 31 October 2018.

11 See <www.theguardian.com/sustainable-business/blog/companies-
embrace-corporate-responsibility-annual-reporting>, accessed
31 October 2018.

12 Davies, 'Guide', para. 6.9. The term 'their members collectively'
refers effectively to a company's shareholders taken as a group;
'external parties' refers to people *other* than the shareholders;
i.e. the other stakeholders apart from shareholders.

13 Ibid., para. 6.35. Davies points out that the list of factors is not
exhaustive.

14 For a very constructive exploration of many factors that are relevant
to the scope for companies to have deep-rooted values that can be
applied in their practice, see Colin Mayer, *Firm Commitment: Why
the Corporation Is Failing Us and How to Restore Trust in It* (Oxford:
Oxford University Press, 2014).

15 Adam Smith (1776), *An Inquiry into the Nature and Causes of the
Wealth of Nations* (Oxford: Clarendon, 1869), vol. 1, bk. 1, ch. 2.

16 Adam Smith also argued strongly for the importance of *morality*
in economic dealings. That is plain from his first major book *The
Theory of Moral Sentiments*, published several decades *before* the
Wealth of Nations. The two books belong together. So if someone
wants to find justification for some view whereby 'market forces'
and an amoral or immoral 'dog eats dog' world amount to the same
thing, then they will have to find a source *other than* Adam Smith.

17 This commandment was itself given by God through Moses; see
Lev. 19:18.

18 In the terms of economic analysis they may have a degree of 'oligopoly' power (where a small number of firms dominate the product market), or monopoly power (one firm dominates). The case of 'monopolistic competition' (many small producers, each with a slightly differentiated product) – similar to 'imperfect competition' – may also offer some scope for variation in the level of wages paid, depending on the circumstances.

19 The growth of companies such as Uber and Deliveroo exemplifies some of these new trends.

20 And/or 'short selling': which is where shares not owned by one party are sold; in particular, where one party *borrows* shares from another, in the expectation that the share price will fall, and thus with a view to buying back the share, after its price has fallen; this trader is hence expecting to make a profit via these trades.

21 Colin Mayer, *Firm Commitment: Why the Corporation Is Failing Us and How to Restore Trust in It* (Oxford: Oxford University Press, 2014), p. 201; emphasis added. Mayer is the Peter Moores Professor of Management Studies at the Said Business School, University of Oxford.

22 Source: Chartered Institute of Personnel and Development and High Pay Centre, 'Executive Pay: Review of FTSE 100 Executive Pay Packages', *Research Report*, August 2017, <www.cipd.co.uk/knowledge/strategy/reward/executive-pay-ftse-100>, accessed 6 November 2018.

23 Source: ibid.

24 Source: Economic Policy Institute, <www.epi.org/publication/ceo-pay-continues-to-rise/>, accessed 3 April 2018.

25 There was an explosion of academic articles from 1992 onwards on the topic of corporate executive pay, many attempting to understand the causes of the new and remarkably large upwards trend.

26 The direction of cause and effect between these two things is much more difficult to evaluate.

27 Patrick Jenkins, 'How Paying Chief Executives Less Can Help Corporate Performance', *Financial Times*, 13 February 2017, <www.ft.com/content/10952312-ee30-11e6-930f-061b01e23655>, accessed 26 March 2018.

28 E.g. 'Neither Rigged Nor Fair: Bosses' Pay in the Rich World Is Not a Fix, but It Is Flawed', *Economist*, 25 June 2016.

29 Jeremy Bowyer, <www.christiantoday.com/article/are.christians. allowed.to.get.rich.billionaire.christian.shares.his.view.on.business. and.making.money/107974.htm>, accessed 5 February 2019.

6 Banks and other financial institutions

1 The words of Jesus Christ, recorded in Matt. 6:24 (NIV 2011).

2 These quotations are from the website of, no less, the International Monetary Fund (IMF), <www.imf.org/external/np/exr/center/mm/ eng/mm_dt_01.htm>, accessed 7 November 2018.

3 The (euphemistic) reference, regarding 'sub-prime' lending, is to mortgages made available to borrowers whose ability to repay was lower than that of typical mortgage borrowers.

4 Risk is measured (assessed) in numerical/statistical terms; clearly, these measures can only be *estimates*, as no one knows the future, and all one can do is measure the risk as carefully as possible.

5 One of the features of many Western economies in recent decades has been a huge increase in the amount of borrowing taken on by firms and corporations (not only individuals and households). Many factors have helped bring this about. But plenty of companies have found the loans (and resultant debts) to be unsustainable. They clearly carry some moral responsibility for their actions. The Jubilee Centre (based in Cambridge), and writers associated with it, have done a lot of helpful work on this. See e.g. the chapters by Paul Mills on 'Economy' and 'Finance' in Michael Schluter and John Ashcroft (eds.), *Jubilee Manifesto: A Framework, Agenda and Strategy for Christian Social Reform* (Leicester: Inter-Varsity Press, 2005), pp. 196–216, 216–233. I do not agree with Mills about the OT ban on interest applying to *all* loans – either then or now – but his analysis of the huge increase in borrowing and debt is very significant. See also Paul Mills's *Cambridge Paper*, March 2011, 'The Great Financial Crisis: A Biblical Diagnosis', <www.jubilee-centre.org/ the-great-financial-crisis-a-biblical-diagnosis-by-paul-mills>, accessed 8 November 2018.

6 Andrew Hartropp, 'The Current Economic and Financial Crisis: Where Are We Now?', *Ethics in Brief*, 16.2 (summer 2010), <www.klice.usertest.mws3.csx.cam.ac.uk/uploads/Ethics%20in%20Brief/Hartropp%20v16.2%20pub.pdf>, accessed 6 November 2018.

7 This is plain from Deut. 15:1, 9–10. Nor was this limited only to a few debts. As Roland de Vaux says, 'The general and periodic nature of this institution is confirmed by Dt. 31:10–11, which orders the reading of the Law "every seven years, the time fixed for the year of remission"' (*Ancient Israel: Its Life and Institutions* [London: DLT, 1973], p. 174). Slaves were also to be released in that seventh year, as taught in the verses that follow on immediately from the teaching on debt cancellation (i.e. Deut. 15:12–15); we should bear in mind that slavery – 'bonded service' – would often have occurred in the first place on account of unpayable debts. So all this teaching holds together as a package.

8 *Life on Debt Row*, <www.rsph.org.uk/uploads/assets/uploaded/75b46b96-10e8-48a3-bc597f3d65d91566.pdf>, accessed 12 November 2018.

9 See <www.theguardian.com/business/2014/dec/16/wonga-cuts-cost-borrowing-interest-rate>, accessed 13 November 2018.

10 Ibid.

11 See e.g. *Life on Debt Row*.

12 Andrew Bailey, 'High-Cost Credit: What Next?', speech published 2 May 2018; <www.fca.org.uk/news/speeches/high-cost-credit-what-next>, accessed 13 November 2018.

13 Ibid.

14 Ibid.

15 See <www.grameenfoundation.org/muhammad-yunus>, accessed 10 October 2018.

16 In Andrew Bailey's speech noted above he included the following: 'We [the FCA] are also exploring the development and scale of provision of alternatives to high-cost credit. The key issues here are: challenges in accessing sustainable capital for alternative credit providers; building a critical mass of support for such approaches, which remain today too much on the fringes; encouraging an appropriate risk appetite and cost recovery for lenders; and helping

social landlords assist tenants to find alternative sources of credit to acquire essential goods; among other points' ('High-Cost Credit').

17 See <www.reuters.com/article/us-usa-economy-geithner-idUSBRE83P01P20120426>, accessed 14 November 2018.

18 Lucy O'Carroll (Chief Economist, Aberdeen Asset Management), 'Hubris and Nemesis: Financial Crisis Insights', <www.aberdeenstandard.com/en-us/us/investor/insights-thinking-aloud/article-page/hubris-and-nemesis-insights-into-the-financial-crisis>, accessed 14 November 2018.

19 My definition is essentially the same as the definitions offered by dictionaries; e.g. 'Intense and selfish desire for something, especially wealth, power or food', <www.en.oxforddictionaries.com/definition/greed>, accessed 14 November 2018; 'A very strong wish to continuously get more of something, especially food or money', <www.dictionary.cambridge.org/dictionary/english/greed>, accessed 14 November 2018.

20 A helpful review is G. J. Pigott, 'Covetousness', in David J. Atkinson and David H. Field, *New Dictionary of Christian Ethics and Pastoral Theology* (Leicester: Inter-Varsity Press, 1995), pp. 267–268.

21 C. S. Lewis, *Mere Christianity* (Glasgow: Collins/Fount, 1955), p. 106.

22 'Fool' translates the word *kĕsîl*; see Derek Kidner, *Proverbs*, TOTC (Leicester: Inter-Varsity Press, 1964), p. 40; emphases original.

23 Richard Layard, 'Happiness and Public Policy: A Challenge to the Profession', *Economic Journal* 116.510 (2006), C24–C33.

24 Ibid.

25 In Rom. 1:18 (the verse that begins the section from vv. 18 to 32) the word often translated in English as 'wickedness' ('the godlessness and wickedness of people') is *adikia*, the exact opposite and negation of the 'justice' and 'righteousness' (*dikaios*) that characterize God in all his ways, and that he commands of us.

26 This becomes clear towards the end of this section (oracle), v. 18. We looked at this whole passage back in chapter 2, and noted the close link between doing justice and concern for the poor and needy. But here we are focusing on what this passage tells us about greed and pride, and how these link to *injustice*.

27 See a piece in the *Financial Times*, 30 August 2018, entitled 'Wonga
Collapses After Surge of Customer Complaints', <www.ft.com/
content/df6bcbdc-ac2a-11e8-89a1-e5de165fa619>, accessed
12 November 2018.

7 Wider society: nationally and globally

1 For a recent argument along these lines, by a Christian theologian
and economist, see Wayne Grudem and Barry Asmus, *The Poverty
of Nations: A Sustainable Solution* (Wheaton: Crossway, 2013),
e.g. pp. 210–211; emphasis original.

2 See <www.worldbank.org/en/news/press-release/2018/09/19/
decline-of-global-extreme-poverty-continues-but-has-slowed-
world-bank>, accessed 20 November 2018.

3 The figures are for 2015. By the way, the use of 'less than $1.90 a day'
as the measure for extreme poverty was adopted by the World Bank
in 2015. Before then the figure was $1.25 a day (and before that $1
a day). This change was made for sound reasons; see <www.blogs.
worldbank.org/developmenttalk/international-poverty-line-has-
just-been-raised-190-day-global-poverty-basically-unchanged-how-
even>, accessed 20 November 2018.

4 Thomas Piketty, *Capital in the Twenty-First Century* (Cambridge,
Mass.: Harvard University Press, 2014).

5 The data here are drawn from a helpful and concise summary of
Piketty's book by Jesper Roine, *Pocket Piketty* (London: Zed, 2017),
p. 35.

6 At this point the CEJ cited Piketty's book as part of its evidence;
Commission on Economic Justice, *Prosperity and Justice*, p. 14.
See <www.ippr.org/research/publications/prosperity-and-justice>,
accessed 30 October 2018.

7 CEJ, *Prosperity and Justice*, 'Executive Summary', p. 8, <www.ippr.
org/research/publications/prosperity-and-justice-executive-
summary>, accessed 30 October 2018.

8 This point may not apply, perhaps, at the extremes of that spectrum:
full-on state-run communism (at one extreme) and fascism (at the
other extreme) may clash so fundamentally with biblical principles
and norms that it would be very difficult to see much scope for

greater economic justice, for a society as a whole, while such regimes were in place. But very few countries in today's world are at either of these extremes.

9 Michael Rhodes and Robby Holt with Brian Fikkert, *Practicing the King's Economy: Honoring Jesus in How We Work, Earn, Spend, Save and Give* (Grand Rapids: Baker, 2018).

10 Ibid., p. 168.

11 Ibid., pp. 172–173. Some people – as Rhodes, Holt and Fikkert note – have raised questions as to whether or not the Jubilee year was ever observed. Clearly, the question as to whether or not the Jubilee was ever observed is of some importance – but this is not the place to explore that. Ultimately, however, that question is much less important than the reality that the Jubilee was plainly commanded by God. As Rhodes and his fellow authors say, 'God commanded it, and it was to be obeyed. Period.' (Rhodes, Holt and Fikkert, *Practicing the King's Economy*, n. 9, p. 301).

12 Unless the 'vision' is 100% equality – but today very few are arguing for *that*.

13 Later in Israel's history Nehemiah was a leader who demonstrated the justice-doing qualities required of a king. See e.g. his actions described in Neh. 5.

14 My friend Desta helped to establish this important work.

15 The quotation is from an encyclical written by Pope Pius XI, *Quadragesimo Anno* (London: Catholic Truth Society, 1931), p. 37; emphasis added. The term 'help' in the statement is the translation offered of the Latin word *subsidium* in the original Latin version. This quotation is itself cited in another, later and very influential, publication in the CST mainstream: National Conference of Catholic Bishops, *Economic Justice for All: Pastoral Letter on Catholic Social Teaching and the U.S. Economy* (Washington, DC: United States Catholic Conference, 1986).

16 See <www.worldbank.org/en/news/press-release/2018/09/19/decline-of-global-extreme-poverty-continues-but-has-slowed-world-bank>, accessed 20 November 2018.

17 Martin Wolf, *Financial Times* economics commentator, wrote an important assessment of globalization, first published in 2004.

This was fourteen years *before* the World Bank's recent data – which I quoted in the main text – which show continued falls in extreme poverty since the early 2000s. Having carefully reviewed the evidence on reductions in extreme poverty, Wolf writes, 'What is more than merely plausible is the proposition that, where numbers in extreme poverty have declined, the cause has been accelerated [economic] growth. This is as true of regions within countries (where mobility is hindered, as in China) as among them' (*Why Globalization Works* [New Haven: Yale Nota Bene, 2005], p. 163). Globalization is a key factor in all of this.

18 See <www.worldbank.org/en/research/brief/poverty-and-shared-prosperity-2018-piecing-together-the-poverty-puzzle-frequently-asked-questions>, accessed 22 November 2018. This report gives the full data to which the speech by the World Bank Group President – which I quoted in the main text – refers.

19 For a way into these debates, compare Wolf's book with that of Joseph E. Stiglitz, *Globalization and Its Discontents* (New York: Norton, 2003). Much has been written since then about globalization, but those two books give a good indication of some of the main issues and areas of dispute.

Resources

Many resources are available to help us as disciples of Jesus Christ do justice in economic life. The list here is intended only to be indicative, not exhaustive.

United Kingdom

The Centre for Enterprise, Markets and Ethics (CEME)

Based in Oxford, the CEME is a company limited by guarantee and a registered charity researching on the interface of Christian theology, economics and business. On its website it says:

> The Centre's distinctive position is that we bring the values of faith to the enterprise economy and the value of the enterprise economy to faith.
>
> CEME's contribution comes from the promotion of the market economy from a Christian perspective within a framework of calling, integrity and ethical behaviour leading to the transformation of business enterprise and contributing to the relief of poverty. (See <www.theceme.org/about-us>, accessed 11 April 2019.)

Christians Against Poverty (CAP)

CAP is a Christian-based charity that runs a debt centre network across the UK. Over recent years it has expanded its services to tackle the causes of debt and poverty too. CAP's website says:

> As well as CAP Debt Help, we now help people step into employment through CAP Job Clubs, help people get control of their habitual dependencies through Fresh Start and a

brand new service, CAP Life Skills, to equip people to live well on a low income. Our vision is to bring freedom and good news to the poor in every community through a nationwide network of CAP projects. (See <www.capuk.org/about-us>, accessed 10 April 2019.)

Jubilee Centre

The Jubilee Centre is a Christian social reform organization that offers a biblical perspective on contemporary issues and underlying trends in society of relevance to the general public. It is based in Cambridge. (See <www.jubilee-centre.org/about-us>, accessed 10 April 2019.)

The Kirby Laing Institute for Christian Ethics (KLICE)

Founded in 2006, KLICE exists to contribute an authentic Christian perspective on biblical, theological and public ethics in the United Kingdom and beyond. It is strategically situated in Tyndale House, with its international reputation for biblical studies, and located at Cambridge University.

Their website says:

Our dream is to develop KLICE, as part of Tyndale House, into a dynamic, international research centre in ethics, opening out into the University, the UK and further afield, which also produces first-rate materials at the accessible, popular level. As such, KLICE will become known for high-level academic work, in the service of the church, and directed towards the flourishing of all creation. (See <www.klice.co.uk/index.php/about>, accessed 11 April 2019.)

The London Institute for Contemporary Christianity (LICC)

On its website LICC says it is

committed to:

- Empowering Christians to make a difference for Christ in our Monday to Saturday lives

- Helping church leaders equip their church communities to do it, and
- Fuelling a movement to reach and renew our nation.

(See <www.licc.org.uk/about>, accessed 10 April 2019.)

Tearfund

Its website says:

> We're Christians passionate about ending poverty. We're following Jesus where the need is greatest, working through local churches to unlock people's potential and helping them to discover that the answer to poverty is within themselves. When disasters strike, we respond quickly. We won't stop until poverty stops.
>
> Tearfund is an evangelical Christian organisation called to reflect the biblical unity of faith and life, of history and eternity, and of the proclamation and demonstration of the gospel. (See <www.tearfund.org> and <www.tearfund.org/about_you/jobs/tearfund_statement_of_faith>, accessed 11 April 2019.)

North America

Cardus

Cardus exists as an independent think tank located in the heart of Canada. Initially founded in 1974 as the 'Work Research Foundation', Cardus emerged from a desire to translate the richness of the Christian faith tradition into the public square for the common good.

On its website it says:

> Determined to live together well in difference and enlarge public conversation on key policy issues, our team works to produce independent research, contribute measured public commentary, and convene projects and initiatives across North America. (See <www.cardus.ca/who-we-are/our-story>, accessed 11 April 2019.)

The Center for Public Justice (CPJ)

On its website it says:

The Center for Public Justice is an independent, nonpartisan organization devoted to *policy research* and *civic education.* Working outside the familiar categories of right and left, conservative and liberal, we seek to help citizens and public officeholders respond to God's call to do justice.

Our mission is to equip citizens, develop leaders, and shape policy in pursuit of our purpose to serve God, advance justice, and transform public life ... The Center bases its research, publications, training, and advocacy work on a comprehensive, Christian political foundation. It was established in 1977 by a group of citizens interested in developing and communicating an integrated biblical view of political service and responsible government. Then, as now, the Center recognized the need to build and uphold a just republic and to promote just relations among the nations. (See www.cpjustice.org/public/page/content/about_us>, accessed 11 April 2019.)

The Chalmers Center for Economic Development

The Chalmers Center equips churches to walk alongside people who are poor, breaking the spiritual, social and material bonds of poverty.

On its website it says:

That transformation is the reason everything we do begins and ends with the church.

Even though the scale of poverty can seem overwhelming, churches of any size can walk alongside people, breaking the bonds of poverty. (See <www.chalmers.org/about>, accessed 11 April 2019.)

The Ezra Institute for Contemporary Christianity (EICC)

Based in Canada, the Ezra Institute was founded in 2009 by Joseph Boot as an evangelical think tank and world view training organization. Boot founded it after years of travelling globally in the work of Christian apologetics and doing significant research in the areas of cultural and mission theology.

On its website it says:

> from its founding, the EICC has understood gospel-centred cultural reformation, beginning with God's own people, as an urgent necessity because the organs and institutions of Western cultural life have been thoroughly saturated by humanistic and increasingly pagan assumptions. These varied religious presuppositions have steadily brought about efforts to redefine the norms of our cultural institutions, unleashing real evils and enchaining Western society in a radical opposition to Christ and the freedom and hope brought by the gospel.

Its study centre on the Niagara Peninsula

> is now the base for our research, writing and publishing, and a strategic venue for the development of new teaching, training and study programs in Christian worldview, cultural apologetics and Christian philosophy. (See <www.ezrainstitute.ca/about/our-story>, accessed 11 April 2019.)

Index of Scripture references

Index of Scripture references

Index of Scripture references

Index of subjects